D0811781

Nigerian Literature:

A Bibliography of Criticism, 1952-1976

*Bibliographies
and
Guides
in
African Studies*

James C. Armstrong
Editor

Nigerian Literature:

A Bibliography of Criticism, 1952-1976

CLAUDIA BALDWIN

G.K.HALL &CO.

70 LINCOLN STREET, BOSTON, MASS.

Library of Congress Cataloging in Publication Data

Baldwin, Claudia A
  Nigerian literature.

  Includes indexes.
  1. Nigerian literature (English)—History and
criticism. I. Title.
PR9387.B34   016.82   80-18715
ISBN 0-8161-8418-6

To my parents

Contents

Introduction

Although Nigerians have been writing on many topics in several languages for centuries, it was not until 1952 that creative works in English were published. That year marked the publication of Amos Tutuola's novel, <u>The Palm-Wine Drinkard</u>, and Dennis Osadebay's volume of poetry, <u>Africa Sings</u>. Since that time the output of creative literature in English has steadily increased and has also received increasing world-wide attention.

This bibliography contains criticism of fifty-one authors and 148 titles. It is a comprehensive compilation of criticism published from 1952 through 1976 of fiction, poetry, and drama of Nigerian authors who have written in English. It includes book reviews, reviews of performances, and critical analyses written in English or French. Citations refer to books, periodical and newspaper articles, essays in books, theses, dissertations, conference papers, and pamphlets. Short annotations are provided when a clearer picture of the subject of the citation seems necessary.

Since this is a bibliography of criticism, not of primary works, not every English-language work of every Nigerian author appears. The bibliography excludes criticism of works written in a language other than English, as well as those that have been translated into English. It also excludes criticism of juvenilia, Onitsha pamphlet literature, and non-fiction. The bibliography is based upon what is available in United States libraries and, therefore, may not include citations to ephemera or periodicals not easily found outside of Nigeria.

The entries are divided into three main parts. In the first are listed the critical works on Nigerian literature in general. The second part lists criticism about Nigerian authors. The authors are listed alphabetically. The criticism of each author is subdivided by general works on the author, where available, criticism of particular works by the author, and by whether the critical work is a criticism, as such, or a review. Book titles are listed in uppercase letters. In upper- and lower-case letters are listed poems, short stories, and plays which either have not been published or have been published in a collection. The last part lists criticisms of anthologies of Nigerian literature. Throughout, the designations Dissertation and Thesis refer to Doctoral dissertations and Master's theses.

I wish to acknowledge the resources of the University Research Library at UCLA and, especially, the Melville J. Herskovits Library of African Studies at Northwestern University, where I was able to find most of the material listed herein.

Periodicals Cited

A B Bookman's Weekly	Clifton, N.J.
Abbia	Yaoundé, Cameroon
Afras Review	Sussex, Eng.
Africa: International Business, Economic and Political Monthly	London
Africa: Journal of the International African Institute	London
Africa in Soviet Studies	Moscow
Africa Quarterly	New Delhi
Africa Report	Washington, D.C.
Africa Today	Denver
Africa Woman	London
African Affairs	London
African Arts/Arts d'Afrique	Los Angeles
African Book Publishing Record	Oxford
African Forum	New York
African Horizon	Zaria, Nigeria
African Literature Today	New York
African Notes	Ibadan, Nigeria
African Statesman	Lagos, Nigeria
African Studies Association of the West Indies Bulletin	Kingston, Jamaica
African Studies Review	Waltham, Mass.
African Writer	Onitsha, Nigeria
Africana Library Journal	New York
Afrique	Casablanca, Morocco
L'Afrique Actuelle	Paris
L'Afrique Littéraire et Artistique	Paris
Afriscope	Lagos, Nigeria
America	New York
American Imago	Detroit
American Scholar	Washington, D.C.
Annales de l'Université d'Abidjan	Abidjan, Ivory Coast
Annales de l'Université de Brazzaville	Brazzaville, Congo
Antiquarian Bookman	Clifton, N.J.
Archiv Orientalni	Prague
Ariel	Calgary, Alta.

Periodicals Cited

Asemka	Cape Coast, Ghana
Atlantic Monthly	Boston
Ba Shiru	Madison, Wis.
Ball State University Forum	Muncie, Ind.
The Benin Review	Benin City, Nigeria
Best Sellers	Scranton, Pa.
Biafra Review	Cambridge, Eng.
Bingo	Dakar, Senegal
Black Academy Review	Bloomfield, N.J.
Black Books Bulletin	Chicago
Black Orpheus	Lagos, Nigeria
Black Times	Palo Alto, Calif.
Black World	Chicago
Booklist	Chicago
Books Abroad	Norman, Okla.
Books and Bookmen	London
Books for Africa	Nairobi, Kenya
Bulletin of Black Theatre	Washington, D.C.
Bulletin of the Association for African Literature in English	Freetown, Sierra Leone
Bulletin of the Association for Commonwealth Literature and Language Studies	Kampala, Uganda
Busara	Nairobi, Kenya
C L A Journal	Baltimore, Md.
Cahiers d'Études Africaine	Paris
Canadian Forum	Toronto
Central African Examiner	Salisbury, Rhodesia
Chicago Review	Chicago
Choice	Middletown, Conn.
Christian Science Monitor	Boston
The Classic	Johannesburg
Commonweal	New York
Comparative Drama	Kalamazoo, Mich.
Comparative Literature Studies	Urbana, Ill.
Compass	Kutztown, Pa.
Concerning Poetry	Bellingham, Wash.
The Conch	Austin, Tex.
Congo-Afrique	Kinshasa, Zaire
Contemporary Review	London
Critique	Atlanta
Crux: A Journal on the Teaching of English	Pretoria
Cultural Events in Africa	Cambridgeshire, Eng.
The Daily Telegraph	London
Daily Times	Lagos, Nigeria
Dhana	Kampala, Uganda
Drama: The Quarterly Theatre Review	London
Drum	Lagos, Nigeria
Drum	Amherst, Mass.
East Africa Journal	Nairobi, Kenya

Eastern Nigeria School Libraries Association Bulletin	Enugu, Nigeria
Education	Benin City, Nigeria
Educational Theatre Journal	Washington, D.C.
English: The Magazine of the English Association	London
English Department Workpapers	Cape Coast, Ghana
English in Africa	Grahamstown, South Africa
English Journal	Urbana, Ill.
English Studies	Amsterdam
English Studies in Africa	Johannesburg
Etudes Anglaises	Paris
Le Français au Nigeria	Ibadan, Nigeria
Genre	Chicago
Ghana Teacher's Journal	Accra, Ghana
Greenfield Review	Greenfield Center, N.Y.
The Guardian	Manchester
The Guardian Weekly	Manchester
Holiday	Indianapolis
The Hollins Critic	Hollins, Va.
Hudson Review	New York
Ibadan	Ibadan, Nigeria
Ikorok	Nsukka, Nigeria
Indigo	New York
Insight	Lagos, Nigeria
International Fiction Review	Fredericton, N.B.
Interlink	Lagos, Nigeria
Iowa Review	Iowa City, Iowa
Issue	Waltham, Mass.
Jeune Afrique	Paris
Joliso	Nairobi, Kenya
Journal of African Studies	Los Angeles
Journal of American Folklore	Austin, Tex.
Journal of Black Studies	Beverly Hills, Calif.
Journal of Canadian Fiction	Montreal
Journal of Commonwealth and Comparative Politics	London
Journal of Commonwealth Literature	London
Journal of Developing Areas	Macomb, Ill.
Journal of Modern African Studies	London
Journal of Popular Culture	Bowling Green, Ohio
Journal of the New African (and the Arts)	Stanford, Calif.
Journal of the Nigeria English Studies Association	Ile-Ife, Nigeria
Kirkus Reviews	New York
Les Langues Modernes	Paris
Legon Observer	Legon, Ghana
Library Journal	New York
The Listener	London
Literary Criterion	Mysore, India

The Literary Half-Yearly	Mysore, India
Literature East and West	Austin, Tex.
London Magazine	London
Lotus: Afro-Asian Writings	Cairo
Mawazo	Kampala, Uganda
The Mirror	Zaria, Nigeria
Modern Drama	Lawrence, Kansas
Modern Language Quarterly	Seattle, Wash.
Moderna Spraak	Stockholm
Ms.	New York
The Muse	Nsukka, Nigeria
Nation	New York
National Observer	Chicoppe, Mass.
Ndaanan	Bathurst, Gambia
Negro American Literature Forum	Terre Haute, Ind.
Negro Digest	Chicago
Negro History Bulletin	Washington, D.C.
The New African	London
New Letters	Kansas City, Mo.
New Society	London
New Statesman	London
New Theatre Magazine	Bristol, Eng.
New York Herald Tribune	New York
New York Times	New York
New York Times Book Review	New York
New Yorker	New York
Nexus	Nairobi, Kenya
Nigeria Magazine	Lagos, Nigeria
Nigerian Field	London
Nigerian Libraries	Ibadan, Nigeria
Nigerian Opinion	Ibadan, Nigeria
Nigerian Student's Voice	Baltimore
Observer	London
Obsidian	Fredonia, N.Y.
Odi	Zomba, Malawi
Odu	Ile-Ife, Nigeria
Oduma	Port Harcourt, Nigeria
Okike	Enugu, Nigeria
Omaba	Nsukka, Nigeria
Paideuma	Orono, Me.
Pan-African Journal	Nairobi, Kenya
Pan Africanist	Evanston, Ill.
La Pensée	Paris
Philologica Pregensia	Prague
Phylon	Atlanta
Plays and Players	London
Poetry	Chicago
Poetry Review	London
Prairie Schooner	Lincoln, Neb.
Présence Africaine	Paris
Publishers Weekly	New York
Punch	London

Periodicals Cited

Quadrant	Sydney
Queen's Quarterly	Kingston, Ont.
Renaissance Two	New Haven
The Reporter	New York
Research in African Literatures	Austin, Tex.
Review of English Literature	Calgary, Alta.
Revue de Littérature Comparée	Paris
Revue des Langues Vivantes	Brussels
Revue Générale Belge	Brussels
Revue Nouvelle	Brussels
San Francisco Chronicle	San Francisco
Sarah Lawrence Journal	Bronxville, N.Y.
Saturday Review	New York
School Library Journal	New York
The Sewanee Review	Sewanee, Tenn.
Shantih	Brooklyn
S'ketsh'	Johannesburg
Something	Addis Ababa
South Atlantic Quarterly	Durham, N.C.
Southern Humanities Review	Auburn, Ala.
Southern Review	Baton Rouge, La.
Spear	Lagos, Nigeria
Spectator	London
Spectrum	Atlanta
Stand	Newcastle, Eng.
Studia Romanica et Anglica	Zagreb
Studies in Black Literature	Fredericksburg, Va.
Studies in the Novel	Denton, Tex.
Time	New York
Time and Tide	London
Times	London
Times Educational Supplement	London
Times Literary Supplement	London
Times Weekly Review	London
Topic	Washington, D.C.
Transition	Kampala, Uganda
Triquarterly	Evanston, Ill.
Twentieth Century	London
Ufahamu	Los Angeles
Umma	Dar Es Salaam, Tanzania
Universitas	Accra, Ghana
Université de Dakar Annales de la Faculté des Lettres et Sciences Humaines	Dakar
The University Review	Kansas City, Mo.
Virginia Quarterly Review	Charlottesville, Va.
West Africa	London
West Africa Link	Lagos, Nigeria
West African Journal of Education	London
West African Religion	Nsukka, Nigeria
West African Review	Liverpool
Western Folklore	Los Angeles

Periodicals Cited

Wilson Library Bulletin	Bronx, N.Y.
Work in Progress	Zaria, Nigeria
World	New York
World Literature Written in English	Arlington, Tex.
Yale French Studies	New Haven
Yale/Theatre	New Haven
Yardbird Reader	Berkeley, Calif.
Zuka	Nairobi, Kenya

Bibliography

Criticism of
Nigerian Literature in General

1 ABASIEKONG, DAN. "Has the Nigerian Novel Run Out of Steam?"
   Drum (Nigerian ed.), No. 183 (August 1966).
      Repetitive themes in Nigerian novels.

2 ACHEBE, CHINUA. "The African Writer and the Biafran Cause."
   The Conch, 1, No. 1 (March 1969), 8-14. Reprinted in
   Biafra Review, No. 1 (1970), pp. 28-30. Reprinted in his
   Morning Yet on Creation Day. Garden City, N.Y.: Anchor
   Press/Doubleday, 1975, pp. 78-84.
      A political paper which calls for Nigerian writers to
   continue to work actively for the cause of Biafra.

3 ACHEBE, CHINUA. "The Role of the Writer in a New Nation."
   Nigeria Magazine, No. 81 (June 1964), pp. 157-60. Reprinted in Nigerian Libraries, 1, No. 3 (September 1964),
   113-119.
      The social responsibilities of Nigerian writers.

4 ACHEBE, CHINUA. "Where Angels Fear to Tread." Nigeria Magazine, No. 75 (December 1962), pp. 61-62. Reprinted in
   African Writers on African Writing. Edited by G. D.
   Killam. Evanston, Ill.: Northwestern University Press,
   1973, pp. 4-7.
      Western critics of Nigerian literature.

5 ADEDEJI, JOEL A. "Drama as an Approach to the Teaching of
   English Literature." West African Journal of Education,
   14 (1970), 135-39.
      Improvisation used as a teaching tool. Examples used
   are the poems "Abiku" by Clark, Soyinka, and Lekan Oyejide
   and "Ivbie" by Clark.

6 ADEDEJI, JOEL A. "Genesis of African Folkloric Literature."
   Yale French Studies, No. 53 (1976), pp. 5-18.
      Nigerian writers whose works rely upon oral tradition--
   Tutuola, Soyinka, Clark, and others.

7   ADEDEJI, JOEL A. "Oral Tradition and the Contemporary Theater
     in Nigeria." Research in African Literatures, 2, No. 2
     (Fall 1971), 134-49. Reprinted in Lotus: Afro-Asian
     Writings, No. 22 (October-December 1974), pp. 131-41.
          Influence of oral tradition in the works of Soyinka,
     Rotimi, and Yoruba-language playwrights.

8   ADEDEJI, JOEL A. "A Profile of Nigerian Theatre 1960-1970."
     Nigeria Magazine, Nos. 107-109 (December/August 1971),
     pp. 3-14.

9   ADEGBIJI, SEGUN. "The Dilemma of the Satirist." Spear
     (July 1972), pp. 29-30.
          The use of satire by Nigerian playwrights and journal-
     ists, especially Wole Soyinka.

10   ADELUGBA, DAPO. "Nationalism and the Awakening National
     Theatre of Nigeria." Thesis, University of California,
     Los Angeles, 1964.

11   ADELUGBA, DAPO. "Trance and Theater: The Nigerian Expe-
     rience." Ufahamu, 6, No. 2 (1976), 47-61.
          Describes the phenomenon of trance in three Nigerian
     societies and relates it to plays by Clark and Soyinka.

12   ADETUGBO, ABIODUN. "Form and Style." In Introduction to
     Nigerian Literature. Edited by Bruce King. New York:
     Africana, 1972, pp. 173-192.

13   AIG-IMOKHUEDE, MABEL. "On Being a West African Writer."
     Ibadan, No. 12 (June 1961), pp. 11-12.
          Cites problems of lack of critical standards, audience,
     and sensitiveness of the West African public.

14   AMADI, ELECHI. "The Novel in Nigeria." Oduma, 2, No. 1
     (August 1974), 33, 35-37. Reprinted in Afriscope, 4,
     No. 11 (November 1974), 40-41, 43, 45.
          Problems, themes, and politics in Nigerian writing.

15   ARMSTRONG, ROBERT P. "The Characteristics and Comprehension
     of a National Literature--Nigeria." In Proceedings of a
     Conference on African Languages and Literatures Held at
     Northwestern University, April 28-30, 1966. Edited by
     Jack Berry. (ERIC ED 012 826), pp. 117-34.

16   ASTRACHAN, ANTHONY M. "Does It Take One to Know One?"
     Nigeria Magazine, No. 77 (June 1963), pp. 132-133.
          Reply to Achebe's essay, "Where Angels Fear to Tread."
     [4]

17   BANHAM, MARTIN. "The Beginnings of a Nigerian Literature in
      English." Review of English Literature, 3, No. 2 (April
      1962), 88-99.
          Surveys a decade of Nigerian literature beginning with
      Ekwensi.

18   BANHAM, MARTIN. "Nigerian Dramatists in English and the Tra-
      ditional Nigerian Theatre." Journal of Commonwealth Lit-
      erature, No. 3 (July 1967), pp. 97-102. Reprinted as
      "Nigerian Dramatists in English." In Readings in Common-
      wealth Literature. Edited by William Walsh. Oxford:
      Clarendon Press, 1973, pp. 135-41.
          Yoruba folk opera and English-language playwrights like
      Soyinka and Clark who borrow the techniques.

19   BANHAM, MARTIN. "Notes on Nigerian Theatre: 1966." Bulletin
      of the Association for African Literature in English, No. 4
      (March 1966), pp. 31-36.

20   BANHAM, MARTIN. "A Piece That We May Fairly Call Our Own."
      Ibadan, No. 12 (June 1961), pp. 15-18.
          Considers Nigerian literature as an imitation of English
      literature, just beginning to develop its own personality.

21   BANHAM, MARTIN and JOHN RAMSARAN. "West African Writing."
      Books Abroad, 36, No. 4 (Autumn 1962), 371-74.

22   BEIER, ULLI. "Nigerian Literature." Nigeria Magazine,
      No. 66 (October 1960), pp. 212-28.

23   BEIER, ULLI. "Quelques poetes nigeriens." Présence Africaine,
      Nos. 32-33 (June-September 1960), pp. 183-86. "Some
      Nigerian Poets." Présence Africaine, English ed., 4-5
      (1960), 50-53.
          Poets writing before 1954 and the younger ones: Mabel
      Imoukhuede, Soyinka, Okara, and Clark.

24   BERRIAN, ALBERT H. "Aspects of the West African Novel." CLA
      Journal, 14, No. 1 (September 1970), 35-41.
          Includes aspects of Achebe's and Ekwensi's novels.

25   BODUNRIN, A. "Literature and the Civil War." African States-
      man, 4, No. 3 (1969), 8-11.
          Rues the fact that "nothing of any literary merit has
      been written on the [Nigerian] war."

26   BONNEAU, DANIELLE. "Le Pidgin English comme moyen d'expres-
      sion littéraire chez les romanciers du Nigéria." Annales
      de l'Université d'Abidjan, 5D (1972), 5-29.
          Pidgin English, especially as used in the novels of
      Achebe and Ekwensi.

27 CHAMPION, ERNEST A. "The Contribution of English Language
and West African Literature to the Rise of National Con-
sciousness in West Africa." Dissertation, Bowling Green
State University, 1974.

28 CHINWEIZU, ONWUCHEKWA JEMIE and IHECHUKWU MADUBUIKE. "Towards
the Decolonization of African Literature." Okike, No. 6
(December 1974), pp. 11-27; No. 7 (April 1975), pp. 65-81.
Reprinted in Transition, 9, No. 48 (April/June 1975),
29-37, 54, 56-57.
    Critical of various Nigerian poets for a failure in
craft and of critics for not recognizing the failure.
Calls for a change in technique, theme, and language.

29 CHUKWUKERE, B. I. "The Problem of Language in African Creative Writing." African Literature Today, No. 3 (1969),
pp. 15-26.

30 CLARK, EBUN. "The Nigerian Theatre and the Nationalist Movement: Part III." Nigeria Magazine, Nos. 115-116 (December
1974), pp. 24-33.

31 CLARK, JOHN PEPPER. "Aspects of Nigerian Drama." Nigeria
Magazine, No. 89 (June 1966), pp. 118-26. Reprinted in his
The Example of Shakespeare. Evanston, Ill.: Northwestern
University Press, 1970, pp. 79-96. Reprinted in African
Writers on African Writing. Edited by G. D. Killam.
Evanston, Ill.: Northwestern University Press, 1973,
pp. 19-32.
    Traditional and modern drama.

32 CLARK, JOHN PEPPER. "Note sur la poésie nigérienne." Présence Africaine, No. 58 (1966), pp. 56-66. "A Note on
Nigerian Poetry." Présence Africaine, English ed., 30
(1966), 55-64. Reprinted as "The Communication Line Between Poet and Public." African Forum, 3, No. 1 (Summer
1967), 42-53. Reprint of "The Communication Line Between
Poet and Public." In his The Example of Shakespeare.
Evanston, Ill.: Northwestern University Press, 1970,
pp. 61-75.
    The line of communication between poet and audience is
less direct with recent written poetry than with earlier
oral poetry.

33 COLLINS, HAROLD R. "The Novel in Nigeria." In Writers the
Other Side of the Horizon: A Guide to Developing Literatures of the World. Edited by Priscilla Tyler. Champaign,
Ill.: National Council of Teachers of English, 1964,
pp. 51-58.

34 CORCORAN, KATHLEEN G. "A Critical Study of Nigerian Litera-
    ture in Relation to Its Background." Thesis, Marshall
    University, 1966-1967.

35 CROWDER, MICHAEL. "Tradition and Change in Nigerian Litera-
    ture." <u>Bulletin of the Association for African Literature
    in English</u>, No. 3 (November 1965), pp. 1-17. Reprinted in
    <u>Triquarterly</u>, No. 5 (1966), pp. 117-28.
        Nigeria's writers face problems in trying to reconcile
    traditional oral literature with a modern approach.

36 CURREY, JAMES. "New Writing after the War." <u>The Guardian</u>
    (30 September 1974), p. 16.

37 DATHORNE, O. R. "West African Novelists in English." In his
    <u>The Black Mind: A History of African Literature</u>.
    Minneapolis: University of Minnesota Press, 1974,
    pp. 156-210.

38 DATHORNE, O. R. "Writing from Nigeria." <u>Bulletin of the
    Association for African Literature in English</u>, No. 1
    (1964?), pp. 31-32.
        A survey of recent publications.

39 DRAYTON, ARTHUR D. "The Return to the Past in the Nigerian
    Novel." <u>Ibadan</u>, No. 10 (November 1960), pp. 27-30.
        Ambivalence towards the past in novels of Ekwensi,
    Tutuola, Aluko, and Achebe.

40 ECHERUO, M. J. C. "Incidental Fiction in Nigeria." <u>African
    Writer</u>, 1, No. 1 (August 1962), 10-11, 18.
        Short story writing.

41 ECHERUO, M. J. C. "Publishing and Writing in Nigeria."
    <u>Afriscope</u>, 5, No. 6 (June 1975), 42-44, 46-47.

42 ECHERUO, M. J. C. "Traditional and Borrowed Elements in
    Nigerian Poetry." <u>Nigeria Magazine</u>, No. 89 (June 1966),
    pp. 142-55.
        Clark, Okigbo, Soyinka, and others use traditional and
    foreign elements in their technique, delivery, subjects,
    and language.

43 EDIBIRI, UNIONMWAN. "La Littérature nigériane contemporaine."
    <u>L'Afrique Littéraire et Artistique</u>, No. 38 (1975),
    pp. 10-21.

44 EDWARDS, PAUL and DAVID R. CARROLL. "Approach to the Novel in
    West Africa." <u>Phylon</u>, 23, No. 4 (Winter 1962), 319-31.
        Assesses Achebe's <u>Things Fall Apart</u> and <u>No Longer at
    Ease</u> and Ekwensi's <u>Jagua Nana</u> in terms of techniques of the
    English novel and proposes that this approach be used with
    West African students.

45   EGEJURU, PHANUEL AKUBUEZE. "The Influence of Audience on
        West African Novels." Dissertation, University of Cali-
        fornia, Los Angeles, 1973.

46   EGUDU, ROMANUS N. "The Nigerian Literary Artist and His
        Society." Ufahamu, 4, No. 1 (Spring 1973), 59-74.
           The role of the artist is discussed using examples from
        the works of Achebe, Okigbo, Soyinka, Ike, and Clark.

47   EGUDU, ROMANUS N. "Nigerian Poets and Nigerian Traditional
        Religion." West African Religion, 16, No. 1 (1975), 1-7.
           Religion in the poetry of Okigbo, Clark, Wonodi, and
        Soyinka.

48   EKWENSI, CYPRIAN. "Problems of Nigerian Writers." Nigeria
        Magazine, No. 78 (September 1963), pp. 217-19.
           Discusses problems of limited Nigerian audience, foreign
        critics, and language.

49   EMENYONU, ERNEST NNEJI. "African Literature: What Does It
        Take to Be a Critic?" African Literature Today, No. 6
        (1973), pp. 1-8.

50   EMENYONU, ERNEST NNEJI. "The Development of Modern Igbo Fic-
        tion, 1857-1966." Dissertation, University of Wisconsin,
        1972.

51   EMENYONU, ERNEST NNEJI. "Post-war Writing in Nigeria."
        African Studies Association annual meeting paper, 1972.
        Issue, 3, No. 2 (Summer 1973), 49-54. Reprinted in Studies
        in Black Literature, 4, No. 1 (Spring 1973), 17-24. Re-
        printed in Ufahamu, 4, No. 1 (Spring 1973), 77-92.
           Works inspired by the war by Ibo writers Achebe,
        Ekwensi, and others.

52   ENEKWE, OSSIE ONUORA. "Theatre in Nigeria: The Modern Vs.
        the Traditional." Yale/Theatre, 8, No. 1 (1976), 62-66.

53   FERGUSON, JOHN. "Nigerian Drama in English." Modern Drama,
        11, No. 1 (May 1968), 10-28.

54   FERGUSON, JOHN. "Nigerian Poetry in English." English, 15,
        No. 90 (Autumn 1965), 231-35. Reprinted in Insight, No. 13
        (July-September 1966), pp. 7-9.
           Themes in the poetry of Osadebay, Aig-Imoukhuede, Segun,
        Clark, Okara, Babalola, Soyinka, and Okigbo.

55   FERGUSON, JOHN. "Nigerian Prose Literature in English."
        English Studies in Africa, 9, No. 1 (March 1966), 43-60.

56   FEUSER, WILLFRIED F. "A Farewell to the Rising Sun: Post-
     Civil War Writings from Eastern Nigeria." Books Abroad,
     49, No. 1 (Winter 1975), 40-49.
          Surveys works by Ibo writers published between 1970 and
     1974.

57   GALPERINA, Y. L. "Under the Sign of Ogun: The Young Writers
     of Nigeria, 1960-1965." In Africa in Soviet Studies:
     Annual 1969. Translated by R. F. Kostiyuk and V. A.
     Epshtein. Moscow: Nauka, 1971, pp. 162-83.
          Okigbo, Clark, Soyinka, Achebe, and Okara.

58   GERARD, ALBERT. "Elégies nigériennes." Revue Générale Belge,
     99 (1963) 37-49.
          Concentrates on Nzekwu's Wand of Noble Wood and Achebe's
     No Longer at Ease.

59   GERARD, ALBERT. "Nigéria: naissance d'une littérature mo-
     derne." Congo-Afrique, No. 22 (February 1968), pp. 66-70.
          Traces the development of modern Nigerian literature.

60   GRAHAM-WHITE, ANTHONY. "West African Drama: Folk, Popular,
     and Literary." Ph.D. thesis, Stanford University, 1969.

61   "The Headline Novels of Africa." West Africa, No. 2360
     (25 August 1962), p. 941.
          The Society of Nigerian Authors (founded by Ekwensi,
     Achebe, Nzekwu, Clark, and Soyinka) submitted this article
     in response to Martin Tucker's article. [159]

62   IKIDDEH, IME. "Literature and the Nigerian Civil War."
     Présence Africaine, No. 98 (1976), pp. 162-74.
          Influence of the war on the works of Achebe, Soyinka,
     and others.

63   IZEVBAYE, D. S. "Nigeria." In Literatures of the World in
     English. Edited by Bruce King. London: Routledge & Kegan
     Paul, 1974, pp. 136-53.

64   IZEVBAYE, D. S. "Politics in Nigerian Poetry." Présence
     Africaine, No. 78 (1971), pp. 143-67.

65   JAHN, JANHEINZ. "L'Exemple du théâtre anglophone et surtout
     nigérian." In Actes du colloque sur le théâtre negro-
     africaine, Abidjan, 1970. Paris: Présence Africaine,
     1971.

66   JONES, ELDRED. "Jungle Drums and Wailing Piano: West African
     Fiction and Poetry in English." African Forum, 1, No. 4
     (Spring 1966), 93-106.
          Influence of two cultures on West African writing.

67 KLÍMA, VLADIMÍR. Modern Nigerian Novels. Dissertationes
    orientales, No. 18. Prague: Czechoslovak Academy of
    Sciences, 1969. 204 pp.

68 KLÍMA, VLADIMÍR. "The Two Literary Centres of Black Africa."
    In Inter-Relations in Asia and Africa. Proceedings of Con-
    ferences held by the Czechoslovak Society for Eastern Stud-
    ies, 1969. Dissertationes orientales, No. 23. Prague:
    Czechoslovak Academy of Sciences, 1970, pp. 168-75.
        Comparison of Nigerian and South African literatures and
    the milieu from which they arose.

69 KOLADE, CHRISTOPHER. "Looking at Drama in Nigeria." African
    Forum, 1, No. 3 (Winter 1966), 77-79.
        The development of theatre groups in Nigeria since 1940.
    Expresses a need for a professional national theatre.

70 LAURENCE, MARGARET. "Other Voices." In her Long Drums and
    Cannons. New York: Praeger, 1969, pp. 169-98.
        Interpretative analysis of the works of Aluko, Amadi,
    Nwankwo, Nwapa, Nzekwu, and Okara.

71 LAWSON, WILLIAM VINCENT. "The Western Scar: The Theme of the
    Been-to in West African Fiction." Dissertation, Stanford
    University, 1975.

72 LEOPOLD, WANDA. "Social and Cultural Metamorphosis of Con-
    temporary Africa in the Light of the Birth and Development
    of Nigerian Novel-Writing." Dissertation, University of
    Warsaw, 1968.

73 LINDFORS, BERNTH. "Achebe's Followers." Revue de Littérature
    Comparée, 48, Nos. 3-4 (July-December 1974), 569-89.
        Ibo writers--Nwankwo, Amadi, Nwapa, Uzodinma, Munonye,
    Agunwa--who have been influenced by Achebe's theme and   .
    technique.

74 LINDFORS, BERNTH. "The African Politician's Changing Image
    in African Literature in English." The Journal of Develop-
    ing Areas, 4, No. 1 (October 1969), 13-28.
        African literature has shown a disillusionment with
    politicians since independence. This study focuses on
    Nigerian literature.

75 LINDFORS, BERNTH. "African Vernacular Styles in Nigerian
    Fiction." CLA Journal, 9, No. 3 (March 1966), 265-73.
        Discusses Tutuola's, Achebe's, Okara's, and Nwankwo's
    attempts to develop an African vernacular style in English.

76 LINDFORS, BERNTH. "Approaches to Folklore in African Litera-
      ture." The Conch, 2, No. 2 (September 1970), 102–11. Re-
      printed in his Folklore in Nigerian Literature. New York:
      Africana, 1973, pp. 6–24.
          Discusses the perspectives of critics who study the in-
      fluence of folklore in African literature in English.

77 LINDFORS, BERNTH. "Five Nigerian Novels." Books Abroad, 39,
      No. 4 (Autumn 1965), 411–13.
          Discusses 1964 novels of Okara, Achebe, Nwankwo, Egbuna,
      and Aluko.

78 LINDFORS, BERNTH. "Nigerian Fiction in English 1952–1967."
      Dissertation, University of California, Los Angeles, 1969.

79 LINDFORS, BERNTH. "Nigerian Novels of 1965." Africa Report,
      11, No. 6 (June 1966), 68–69.
          Soyinka's The Interpreters, Nzekwu's Highlife for Liz-
      ards, Ike's Toads for Supper, and Akpan's The Wooden Gong.

80 LINDFORS, BERNTH. "Nigerian Novels of 1966." Africa Today,
      14, No. 5 (October 1967), 27–31.
          Novels by Achebe, Ekwensi, Aluko, Nwapa, Munonye, and
      Amadi are discussed with insight into directions African
      fiction is taking.

81 LINDFORS, BERNTH. "Popular Literature for an African Elite."
      Journal of Modern African Studies, 12, No. 3 (September
      1974), 471–86.
          Overview of secondary school magazines and university
      publications in which many Nigerian writers first got into
      print.

82 LINDFORS, BERNTH. "Shakespeare and Nigerian Drama." Proceed-
      ings of the 6th Congress of the International Comparative
      Literature Association. Stuttgart: Kunst and Wissen,
      Erich Bieber, 1975, pp. 639–41.
          Shakespeare's influence on Nigerian drama.

83 LINDFORS, BERNTH. "Yoruba and Igbo Prose Styles in English."
      Black Orpheus, 2, No. 7 (1971–1972), 21–30. Reprinted as
      "Characteristics of Yoruba and Igbo Prose Styles in Eng-
      lish." In Common Wealth. Edited by Anna Rutherford.
      Aarhus: Akademisk Boghandel, 1972, pp. 47–61. Reprint of
      "Characteristics of Yoruba and Ibo Prose Styles in English."
      In his Folklore in Nigerian Literature. New York:
      Africana, 1973, pp. 153–75.
          Contrasts the styles of Yoruba and Ibo writers.

84 McDANIEL, RICHARD BRYAN. "Some Aspects of Myth in Selected
      Nigerian Works of Literature." Dissertation, University of
      New Brunswick, 1974.

85 McDOWELL, ROBERT E. "The African-English Novel." Disserta-
    tion, University of Denver, 1966.

86 MOORE, GERALD. "The Arts in the New Africa." African Affairs,
    66, No. 263 (1967), 140-48.
        Recent developments in the works of artists like Achebe,
    Clark, and Okigbo.

87 MOORE, GERALD. "Mots anglais, vies africaines." Présence
    Africaine, No. 54 (1965), pp. 116-26. "English Words,
    African Lives." Présence Africaine, English ed., 26
    (1965), 90-101.
        On Achebe, Ekwensi, and Aluko.

88 MOORE, GERALD. "Reintegration with the Lost Self: A Theme in
    Contemporary African Literature." Revue de Littérature
    Comparée, 48 (July-December 1974), 488-503.
        The theme in Okigbo's poetry, Soyinka's The Strong
    Breed, and others.

89 MOORE, JANE ANN. "The Middle Society: Five Orientations to-
    wards Husband-Wife Roles in West African Novels." In
    Seminar Papers on African Studies. Edited by Sulayman
    Sheih Nyang. Washington, D.C.: African Studies & Research
    Program, Howard University, 1974, pp. 85-100.

90 MUNONYE, JOHN. "Book Business in Nigeria: Writing."
    Nigerian Libraries, 2, No. 2 (September 1966), 77-79.
        Themes, language, and audience of Nigerian writing.

91 "A National Theatre for Nigeria?" Drum (Nigeria ed.), No. 196
    (August 1967), pp. 21-24.
        Speculation about Nigerians' appreciation of drama.

92 NGWUBE, ANEROBI. "Nigerian War Literature." Indigo, No. 2
    (January 1974), pp. 3-4, 6-7.

93 "Nigeria at the Commonwealth Festival." Nigeria Magazine,
    No. 87 (1965), pp. 297-303.
        Clark's Song of a Goat and The Masquerade; Soyinka's The
    Road; Ladipo's ObaKoso.

94 NKOSI, LEWIS. "African Literature: Part II: English-
    speaking West Africa." Africa Report, 7, No. 11 (December
    1962), 15-17, 31. Reprinted as "English-speaking West
    Africa: Synthesizing Past and Present." In A Handbook of
    African Affairs. Edited by Helen Kitchen. New York:
    Praeger, 1964, pp. 285-95.

95 NKOSI, LEWIS. "A Release of Energy: Nigeria, the Arts and
Mbari." New African, 1, No. 11 (November 1962), 10-11.
Introduces writers of Nigeria--Okigbo, Clark, Soyinka,
and Tutuola.

96 NOSS, PHILIP A. "The Cruel City." Revue de la Littérature
Comparée, 48, Nos. 3-4 (July-December 1974), 462-74.
The depiction of the city in Nigerian and Cameroonian
novels.

97 OBIECHINA, EMMANUEL. Culture, Tradition and Society in the
West African Novel. New York: Cambridge University Press,
1975. 296 pp.

98 OBIECHINA, EMMANUEL N. "Problem of Language in African Writing: The Example of the Novel." The Conch, 5, Nos. 1-2
(1973), 11-28.
Problem of expressing African concepts in the English
language.

99 OBIECHINA, EMMANUEL N. "Transition from Oral to Literary
Tradition." Présence Africaine, No. 63 (1967), pp. 140-61.

100 NWOGA, DONATUS I. "Plagiarism and Authentic Creativity in
West Africa." Research in African Literatures, 6, No. 1
(Spring 1975), 32-39. Reprinted in Critical Perspectives
on Nigerian Literatures. Edited by Bernth Lindfors.
Washington, D.C.: Three Continents Press, 1975,
pp. 159-67.
Asserts that borrowings from traditional literature do
not constitute plagiarism. The primary example is Okigbo.

101 O'FLINN, J. P. "Towards a Sociology of the Nigerian Novel."
African Literature Today, No. 7 (1975), pp. 34-52.
The social background of the development of the Nigerian
novel and the effect of the civil war on the output.

102 OGUNBA, OYIN. "Modern Drama in West Africa." Black Orpheus,
2, No. 4 (1970), 11-20. Reprinted in Perspectives on
African Literature. Edited by Christopher Heywood. New
York: Africana, 1971, pp. 81-105.
Concerned with themes. Nigerian writers surveyed are
Henshaw, Clark, and Soyinka.

103 OGUNBA, OYIN. "Le Théâtre au Nigéria." Présence Africaine,
No. 58 (1966), pp. 67-90. "Theatre in Nigeria." Présence
Africaine, English ed., 30 (1966), 65-88.

104 OGUNGBESAN, KOLAWOLE. "Literature and Society in West
Africa." Africa Quarterly, 11, No. 3 (October-December
1971), 216-24.

13

105   OGUNGBESAN, KOLAWOLE. "Nigerian Writers and Political Commit-
        ment." Ufahamu, 5, No. 2 (1974), 20-50.
            The thoughts of Okigbo, Clark, and Soyinka on the need
        for political commitment.

106   OKONKWO, JULIET I. "Adam and Eve: Igbo Marriage in the
        Nigerian Novel." The Conch, 3, No. 2 (September 1971),
        137-51.
            Marriage in novels of Nwankwo, Munonye, Amadi, Achebe,
        and Nwapa.

107   OKONKWO, JULIET I. "The Talented Woman in African Litera-
        ture." Africa Quarterly, 15, Nos. 1-2 (April-September
        1975), 36-47.
            Examines women's roles as reflected in Amadi's The Con-
        cubine, Munonye's Obi, Nwapa's Efuru, and Aidoo's Anowa.

108   OKWU, EDWARD C. "A Language of Expression for Nigerian Liter-
        ature." Nigeria Magazine, No. 91 (December 1966),
        pp. 289-92, 313-15.
            English vs. Nigerian languages.

109   OLAFIOYE, TAYO. "Public Poetry of West Africa: A Survey."
        Ufahamu, 6, No. 1 (1975), 74-95.
            Poetry which is shaped by politics.

110   O'MALLEY, P. "Recent Nigerian Fiction." Nigerian Opinion, 3,
        No. 4 (April 1967), 190-92.
            A critical survey.

111   OMOTOSO, KOLE. "The Missing Apex: A Search for an Audience."
        In Publishing in Africa in the Seventies. Edited by
        E. Oluwasanmi, et al. Ile-Ife: University of Ife Press,
        1975, pp. 251-61.
            On the paucity of indigenous publishers for Nigerian
        writers.

112   OMOTOSO, KOLE. "Politics, Propaganda, and Prostitution."
        Afriscope, 4, No. 11 (November 1974), 45, 47, 49.
            Reply to Amadi on writers' political role. [14]

113   OMOTOSO, KOLE. "Politics, Propaganda, and Prostitution of
        Literature." Iowa Review, 7, Nos. 2-3 (1976), 238-45.
            The aim of most of the first generation of Nigerian
        writers was to show outsiders what Africa was like without
        Europeans. A new generation has brought about changes.

114   O'NEAL, JOHN. "Theater in Yorubaland." Black World, 19,
        No. 9 (July 1970), 39-48.
            An Afro-American's impression of the theater, especially
        Ogunmola's "The Palm-Wine Drinkard" and Ola Rotimi's
        "Kurunmi."

115 OSOFISAN, FEMI. "Anubis Resurgent: Chaos and Political
       Vision in Recent Literature." Le Français au Nigeria, 10,
       No. 2 (September 1975), 13–23.
            Examples from Nigerian writers Clark, Soyinka, and
       Omotoso.

116 OSOFISAN, FEMI. "'The Quality of Hurt': A Survey of Recent
       Nigerian Poetry." Afriscope, 4, No. 7 (July 1974), 45–48,
       51–53; 4, No. 9 (September 1974), 46–49, 51, 53–55.
            Okigbo, Clark, Soyinka, and Okara.

117 "Our Authors and Performing Artists." Nigeria Magazine,
       No. 88 (March 1966), pp. 57–64; No. 89 (June 1966),
       pp. 133–40.
            Biographical sketches.

118 PALMER, EUSTACE. "Social Comment in the West African Novel."
       Studies in the Novel, 4, No. 2 (Summer 1972), 218–30.
            Includes Achebe's A Man of the People and Okara's The
       Voice.

119 PANTER-BRICK, S. K. "Fiction and Politics: The African
       Writer's Abdication." The Journal of Commonwealth and
       Comparative Politics, 13, No. 1 (March 1975), 79–86.
            Includes discussion of Mezu's Behind the Rising Sun,
       Achebe's Girls at War and Other Stories, and Okigbo's
       Labyrinths.

120 PARRY, JOHN. "Nigerian Novelists." Contemporary Review, 200
       (July 1961), 377–81.
            Discusses the works of Tutuola, Aluko, Achebe, and
       Ekwensi.

121 POVEY, JOHN F. "Changing Themes in the Nigerian Novel."
       Journal of the New African Literature, No. 1 (Spring 1966),
       pp. 3–11.
            Nigerian writers are beginning to stray from the once
       pervasive theme of culture conflict.

122 POVEY, JOHN F. "Contemporary West African Writing in English."
       Books Abroad, 40, No. 3 (Summer 1966), 253–60.

123 POVEY, JOHN. "The English Language of the Contemporary Afri-
       can Novel." Critique, 11, No. 3 (1969), 79–96.
            The implications of writing in a second language. The
       English usage of Tutuola, Ekwensi, Nwankwo, Okara, and
       Achebe is described.

124 POVEY, JOHN F. "The Nigerian War: The Writer's Eye." Journal
       of African Studies, 1, No. 3 (Fall 1974), 354–60.
            Discusses novels which deal with aspects of the war.

125   POVEY, JOHN F.   "The Political Theme in South and West African
       Novels." Africa Quarterly, 9, No. 1 (April–June 1969),
       33–39. African Studies Association annual meeting paper,
       1965.
            The novels of Ekwensi, Aluko, and Achebe are used as
       examples.

126   POVEY, JOHN F.   "West African Drama in English." Comparative
       Drama, 1, No. 2 (Summer 1967), 110–21.
            Includes contrast of style in Sharif Easmon's Dear Par-
       ent and Ogre and J. P. Clark's Song of a Goat.

127   POVEY, JOHN F.   "West African Poetry: Tradition and Change."
       Africa Today, 15, No. 4 (August/September 1968), 5–7.
            Aspects of dual cultures in West African poetry.

128   PRIEBE, RICHARD.   "Escaping the Nightmare of History: The
       Development of a Mythic Consciousness in West African Lit-
       erature." Ariel: A Review of International English
       Literature, 4, No. 2 (April 1973), 55–67.
            Wole Soyinka, Kofi Awoonor, and Ayi Kwei Armah on a con-
       tinuum beginning with Tutuola.

129   RAMSARAN, J. A.   "African Twilight: Folktale and Myth in
       Nigerian Literature." Ibadan, No. 15 (March 1963),
       pp. 17–19.
            Use of the folktale by Fagunwa, Tutuola, and Achebe.

130   RAVENSCROFT, ARTHUR.   "An Introduction to West African Novels
       in English." The Literary Criterion, 10, No. 2 (Summer
       1972), 38–56.
            Emphasis on Nigerian novels.

131   RAVENSCROFT, ARTHUR.   "The Nigerian Civil War in Nigerian
       Literature." In Commonwealth Literature and the Modern
       World. Edited by Hena Maes-Jelinek. Brussels: Didier,
       1975, pp. 105–13.

132   RAVENSCROFT, ARTHUR.   "Novels of Disillusion." Journal of
       Commonwealth Literature, No. 6 (January 1969), pp. 120–37.
       Reprinted in Readings in Commonwealth Literature. Edited
       by William Walsh. Oxford: Clarendon Press, 1973,
       pp. 186–205.
            Includes Achebe's A Man of the People, Soyinka's The
       Interpreters, and Okara's The Voice.

133   RICARD, ALAIN.   "Nationalisme et littérature du Nigeria:
       1960–1967." L'Afrique Littéraire et Artistique, No. 10
       (1970), pp. 22–27.

134   RICARD, ALAIN. "Le Théâtre entre l'oral et l'écrit au Ghana
      et au Nigeria." Recherche, Pedagogie et Culture, 3, No. 16
      (March-April 1975), 12-20. "Between the Oral and the Writ-
      ten: Theatre in Ghana and Nigeria." Educational Theatre
      Journal, 28, No. 2 (May 1976), 229-38.
          History of popular theatre in Nigeria, including works
      of Soyinka.

135   RIGHT, JOSEPH D. "Why They Are Ibo." Nigeria Magazine,
      No. 81 (June 1964), pp. 83, 160.
          Letter which discusses why Nigeria's leading novelists
      are Ibo.

136   ROSCOE, ADRIAN A. Mother is Gold: A Study in West African
      Literature. Cambridge: University Press, 1971. 273 pp.
          Focuses on Nigeria.

137   ROSCOE, ADRIAN A. "Nigerian Literature in English: Problems
      and Progress." Dissertation, City University of New York
      (Queens), 1968.

138   SCHMIDT, NANCY J. "An Anthropological Analysis of Nigerian
      Fiction." Dissertation, Northwestern University, 1965.

139   SCHMIDT, NANCY J. "Nigerian Fiction and the African Oral Tra-
      dition." Journal of the New African Literature and the
      Arts, Nos. 5-6 (Spring-Fall 1968), pp. 10-19. Reprinted in
      New African Literature and the Arts, vol. 2. Edited by
      Joseph Okpaku. New York: Crowell, 1970, pp. 25-38.
          Plot structure, proverbs, tales and epigrammatic naming
      are elements of oral tradition which appear in Nigerian
      fiction in English.

140   SEVERAC, ALAIN. "Aspect du roman africain anglophone: un
      roman engagé." Les Langues Modernes, 65, No. 3 (May/June
      1971), 82-93.
          Surveys major writers of Nigeria along with South Africa
      and Kenya.

141   SHELTON, AUSTIN J. "The Articulation of Traditional and Mod-
      ern in Igbo Literature." The Conch, 1, No. 1 (March 1969),
      30-52.
          Relates Igbo oral tradition to written literature by
      Igbo writers.

142   SHELTON, AUSTIN J. "Behaviour and Cultural Values in West
      African Stories: Literary Sources for the Study of Cul-
      tural Contact." Africa, 34, No. 4 (October 1964), 353-59.
          Nigerian novels examined are Nzekwu's Wand of Noble
      Wood, Achebe's No Longer at Ease, and Soyinka's The Lion
      and the Jewel.

143 SHELTON, AUSTIN J. "Nationalism and Cosmopolitanism as
        Source-effect and Motif in Modern Nigerian Literature."
        In <u>Proceedings of the IVth Congress of the International
        Comparative Literature Association</u>. Edited by François
        Jost. The Hague: Mouton, 1966, pp. 687-91.
        Ekwensi, Achebe, and Nzekwu are discussed.

144 SOYINKA, WOLE. "From a Common Back Cloth: Reassessment of
        the African Literary Image." <u>American Scholar</u>, 32, No. 3
        (Summer 1963), 387-96.

145 SOYINKA, WOLE. "Neo-Tarzanism: The Poetics of Pseudo-
        Tradition." <u>Transition</u>, 9, No. 48 (April/June 1975),
        38-44.
        Response to Chinweizu and Ihechukwu. [28]

146 STERLING, THOMAS. "Africa's Black Writers." <u>Holiday</u>, 41
        (February 1967), 131-40.
        This survey considers Nigerian writers Soyinka, Tutuola,
        Achebe, and Okara.

147 STEVENSON, W. H. "<u>The Horn</u>: What It Was and What It Did."
        <u>Research in African Literatures</u>, 6, No. 1 (Spring 1975),
        5-31. Reprinted in <u>Critical Perspectives in Nigerian Lit-
        eratures</u>. Edited by Bernth Lindfors. Washington, D.C.:
        Three Continents Press, 1976, pp. 215-41.

148 TAIWO, OLADELE. "Historical and Cultural Influences on the
        Nigerian Novelist." In his <u>Culture and the Nigerian Novel</u>.
        New York: St. Martin's Press, 1976, pp. 1-33.

149 TAIWO, OLADELE. "The Link between Tradition and Modern Expe-
        rience in the Nigerian Novel." <u>Studies in Black Litera-
        ture</u>, 5, No. 3 (Winter 1974), 11-16.
        Attitude toward traditional culture in the works of
        Tutuola, Tafawa Balewa, and Okara.

150 TAIWO, OLADELE. "Nigerian Drama." In his <u>An Introduction to
        West African Literature</u>. New York: Humanities Press,
        1967, pp. 68-83.

151 TAIWO, OLADELE. "The Use of Comedy in Nigerian Fiction." <u>The
        Literary Half-Yearly</u>, 15, No. 2 (July 1974), 107-20.
        The purposes of comedy, especially in Achebe's novels
        and Nwankwo's <u>Danda</u>.

152 THOMAS, PETER. "Great Plenty to Come: A Personal Reminis-
        cence of the First Generation of Nsukka Poets." <u>The Muse</u>,
        No. 4 (May 1972), pp. 5-8.

153　THOMAS, PETER.　"Ibo Poetry in English since the End of the
　　　　Nigerian Civil War."　Books Abroad, 48, No. 1 (Winter
　　　　1974), 34-41.
　　　　　Analyzes the poetry of a group of young poets from
　　　　Nsukka.

154　THOMAS, PETER.　"Voices from Nsukka:　Students and the Art of
　　　　Poetry."　New African, 5, No. 7 (September 1966), 144-45.
　　　　　The author tells of his experiences teaching young poets
　　　　at Nsukka.

155　THOMAS, PETER.　"The Water Maid and the Dancer:　Figures of
　　　　the Nigerian Muse."　Literature East & West, 12, No. 1
　　　　(March 1968), 85-93.
　　　　　Themes in the poetry of Okigbo, Okara, Clark, and
　　　　Wonodi.

156　TIBBLE, ANNE.　"West Africa."　In her African English Litera-
　　　　ture:　A Short Survey and Anthology of Prose and Poetry up
　　　　to 1965.　London:　Peter Owen, 1965, pp. 87-116.

157　TREGIDGO, P. S.　"West African Novels."　Ghana Teacher's
　　　　Journal, No. 39 (July 1963), pp. 17-23.
　　　　　Introduction to Nigerian authors Tutuola, Ekwensi,
　　　　Achebe, and Nzekwu.

158　TUCKER, MARTIN.　"The Headline Novels of Africa."　West
　　　　Africa, No. 2356 (28 July 1962), p. 829.
　　　　　Criticizes African novelists for their obsession with
　　　　social issues.　Achebe, Nzekwu, Ekwensi, Conton, and Aluko
　　　　are given as examples.

159　TUCKER, MARTIN.　"West Africa by Africans."　In his Africa in
　　　　Modern Literature:　A Survey of Contemporary Writing in
　　　　English.　New York:　Frederick Ungar, 1967, pp. 66-127.

160　UKA, KALU.　"Drama in Nigerian Society."　The Muse, No. 5
　　　　(May 1973), pp. 11, 13-15, 36-38.

161　UKA, KALU.　"'English' through Drama."　Journal of the Nigeria
　　　　English Studies Association, 6, No. 2 (December 1974),
　　　　91-99.
　　　　　Describes a unique English language in West African
　　　　drama with examples from Clark and Soyinka.

162　UKA, KALU.　"The Place of Drama as Medium of Mass Expression
　　　　in Nigeria."　The Muse, No. 6 (May 1974), pp. 45-50.

163 VAVILOV, V. "Nigerian Literature and Reality." In Essays on
     African Culture. Edited by M. A. Korostovtsev. Moscow:
     Nauka Publishing House, 1966, pp. 155-63.
       Discusses Western critics' views on Nigerian literature
     and looks at novels by Soyinka, Okara, and Nwankwo.

164 WAKE, CLIVE. "Nigeria, Africa and the Caribbean: A Bird's
     Eye View." In Introduction to Nigerian Literature. Ed-
     ited by Bruce King. New York: Africana, 1972, pp. 193-208.
       Differences and similarities between Nigerian literature
     and black literature from other parts of the world.

165 WREN, ROBERT M. "The Indigenization of English: Rhetoric in
     Modern Nigerian Literature." Submitted to International
     Congress of Africanists, 3d, Addis Ababa, 1973. 22 pp.

166 "Writing in West Africa: A Chance to Adapt and to Experi-
     ment." Times Literary Supplement (10 August 1962), p. 570.
       African and English influences on the language of West
     African writing.

167 YAKUBU, IHKHAZS. "Hope for Nigerian Writers at Last." Daily
     Times [Lagos] (21 April 1962), p. 14.
       On the formation of the Society of Nigerian Authors.

168 YOUNG, PETER. "The Language of West African Literature in
     English." In The English Language in West Africa. Edited
     by John Spencer. London: Longman, 1971, pp. 165-84.

169 YOUNG, PETER. "Mechanism to Medium: The Language of West
     African Literature in English." In Common Wealth. Edited
     by Anna Rutherford. Aarhus: Akademisk Boghandel, 1972,
     pp. 35-46.

170 YOUNG, PETER. "Tradition, Language and the Reintegration of
     Identity in West African Literature in English." In The
     Critical Evaluation of African Literature. Edited by Edgar
     Wright. Washington, D.C.: Inscape, 1976, pp. 23-50.

Criticism of
Nigerian Authors and Their Works

CHINUA ACHEBE

171 ACHEBE, CHINUA. "Named for Victoria, Queen of England." New Letters, 40, No. 1 (Autumn 1973), 14-22. Reprinted in his Morning Yet on Creation Day. Garden City, N.Y.: Anchor Press/Doubleday, 1975, pp. 115-24.
Autobiographical.

172 ADEBAYO, 'TUNJI. "The Writer and the West African Present: Achebe's Crusade Against Cynicism and Apathy." African Studies Association of the West Indies Bulletin, No. 7 (December 1974), pp. 3-16.
Achebe's attitude toward the African present, especially in A Man of the People.

173 "The African Writer in Search of His Audience." Negro Digest, 15, No. 1 (November 1965), 10-17.
Transcript of Lewis Nkosi and Wole Soyinka interview of Achebe for a National Educational Television program.

174 AMADI, LAURENCE EKPEMA. "Historical and Cultural Elements in the Works of Chinua Achebe and Wole Soyinka: Instructional Resources for the Teacher of Nigerian Literature and Culture." Dissertation, University of Missouri, 1972.

175 ANGOGO, R. "Achebe and the English Language." Busara, 7, No. 2 (1975), 1-14.

176 AWOONOR, KOFI. "Chinua Achebe and the Rise of Modern African Fiction." In his The Breast of the Earth. Garden City, N.Y.: Anchor Press/Doubleday, 1975, pp. 251-80.

177 BARTHOLD, BONNIE JO. "Three West African Novelists: Chinua Achebe, Wole Soyinka, and Ayi Kwei Armah." Dissertation, University of Arizona, 1975.

21

Achebe, Chinua

178   BAUGH, LAWRENCE E. "An Interview with Chinua Achebe." <u>Drum</u>,
      5, No. 3 (Spring 1974), 18-22.

179   BENOT, YVES. "Un Romancier nigérien: le réalisme tragique de
      Chinua Achebe." <u>La Pensée</u>, No. 153 (September/October
      1970), pp. 122-30.

180   "<u>Black Books Bulletin</u> Interviews Chinua Achebe." <u>Black Books
      Bulletin</u>, 3, No. 3 (Fall 1975), 20-22.

181   BÖTTCHER, KARL H. "The Narrative Technique in Achebe's
      Novels." <u>Journal of the New African Literature and the
      Arts</u>, Nos. 13-14 (1972), pp. 1-12.

182   BROWN, LLOYD W. "Cultural Norms and Modes of Perception in
      Achebe's Fiction." <u>Research in African Literatures</u>, 3,
      No. 1 (Spring 1972), 21-35. Reprinted in <u>Critical Perspec-
      tives on Nigerian Literatures</u>. Edited by Bernth Lindfors.
      Washington, D.C.: Three Continents Press, 1976, pp. 131-45.
          Western perceptions of Nigerian culture in Achebe's
      novels.

183   BROWN, LLOYD W. "The Historical Sense: T. S. Eliot and Two
      African Writers." <u>The Conch</u>, 3, No. 1 (March 1971), 59-70.
          Studies the impact of Eliot's work on Achebe and James
      Rubadiri, a Malawian.

184   BUTTS, DENNIS. "The Novels of Chinua Achebe." <u>Stand</u>, 8,
      No. 4 (1967), 62-68.

185   CARROLL, DAVID. <u>Chinua Achebe</u>. New York: Twayne, 1970.
      156 pp.

186   CHARGOIS, JOSEPHINE ASBURY. "Two Views of Black Alienation:
      A Comparative Study of Chinua Achebe and Ralph Ellison."
      Dissertation, Indiana University, 1974.

187   "Chinua Achebe on Biafra." <u>Transition</u>, No. 36 [Vol. 7, No. 5]
      (1968), pp. 31-38.
          Interview.

188   CHUKWUKERE, B. I. "The Problem of Language in African Crea-
      tive Writing." <u>African Literature Today</u>, No. 3 (1969),
      pp. 15-26.
          Using Ekwensi and Achebe as examples, this article deals
      with the problems African writers incur by using the Eng-
      lish language.

Achebe, Chinua

189   "Conversation with Chinua Achebe." Africa Report, 9, No. 5
       (July 1964), 19-21.
              Interview by Lewis Nkosi and Wole Soyinka.

190   DALE, JAMES. "Chinua Achebe, Nigerian Novelist." Queen's
       Quarterly, 75, No. 3 (Autumn 1968), 460-75.

191   DUERDEN, DENNIS. "Chinua Achebe." In African Writers Talk-
       ing. Edited by Cosmo Pieterse and Dennis Duerden. New
       York: Africana, 1972, pp. 9-11.
              Interview.

192   ECHERUO, M. J. C. "Chinua Achebe." In A Celebration of Black
       and African Writing. Edited by Bruce A. King and Kolawole
       Ogungbesan. New York: Oxford University Press, 1975,
       pp. 150-63.

193   EKO, EBELE. "Chinua Achebe and His Critics: Reception of His
       Novels in English and American Reviews." Studies in Black
       Literature, 6, No. 3 (Fall 1975), 14-20.

194   EKO, EBELE. "The Critical Reception of Amos Tutuola, Chinua
       Achebe and Wole Soyinka in England and America 1952-1974."
       Dissertation, University of North Carolina at Greensboro,
       1974.

195   No entry

196   EMENYONU, ERNEST and PATRICIA EMENYONU. "Achebe: Accountable
       to Our Society." Africa Report, 17, No. 5 (May 1972), 21,
       23, 25-27.
              Interview.

197   "Entretien avec Chinua Achebe." Afrique, No. 27 (October
       1963), pp. 41-42.

198   FERRIS, WILLIAM R., JR. "Folklore and the African Novelist:
       Achebe and Tutuola." Journal of American Folklore, 86,
       No. 339 (January-March 1973), 25-36.

199   GACHUKIA, EDDAH W. "Chinua Achebe and Tradition." In
       Standpoints on African Literature: Critical Essays. Ed-
       ited by Chris L. Wanjala. Nairobi: East African Litera-
       ture Bureau, 1973, pp. 172-87.

200   GERARD, ALBERT. "Chinua Achebe, chroniqueur des effrondre-
       ments." La Revue Nouvelle, No. 46, pp. 350-53.

Achebe, Chinua

201 GERE, ANNE RUGGLES. "West African Oratory and the Fiction of
       Chinua Achebe and T. M. Aluko." Dissertation, University
       of Michigan, 1974.

202 GITHAE-MUGO, MICERE M. "Visions of Africa in the Fiction of
       Chinua Achebe, Margaret Laurence, Elspeth Huxley and Ngugi
       wa Thiong'o." Dissertation, University of New Brunswick
       (Canada), 1973.

203 GOWDA, H. H. ANNIAH. "The Novels of Chinua Achebe." The Lit-
       erary Half-Yearly, 14, No. 2 (July 1973), 3-9.

204 GRIFFITHS, GARETH. "Language and Action in the Novels of
       Chinua Achebe." African Literature Today, No. 5 (1971),
       pp. 88-105.

205 HADDAD, MARJORIE ARLENE. "Pollution and Purification in the
       Novels and Plays of Wole Soyinka, Chinua Achebe, and John
       Pepper Clark." Dissertation, New York University, 1976.

206 HAMILTON, ALEX. "African Explorer." The Guardian
       (28 February 1972), p. 8.
          Biographical.

207 HEDBERG, JOHANNES. "Chinua Achebe--A Presentation." Moderna
       Sprak, 58, No. 4 (1964), 435-38.
          Introduction to Achebe and his works.

208 IKE, ROSALINE. "Tragedy and Social Purpose: The Novels of
       Chinua Achebe." Something, No. 5 (April 1966), pp. 3-13.

209 INNES, CATHERINE LYNETTE. "Through the Looking Glass:
       Achebe, Synge and Cultural Nationalism." Dissertation,
       Cornell University, 1973.

210 "Interview with Chinua Achebe." In Palaver: Interviews with
       Five African Writers in Texas. Edited by Bernth Lindfors,
       et al. Austin: African & Afro-American Research Insti-
       tute, University of Texas, 1972, pp. 4-12.

211 IRELE, ABIOLA. "Chinua Achebe: The Tragic Conflict in
       Achebe's Novels." Black Orpheus, No. 17 (June 1965),
       pp. 24-32. Reprinted in Introduction to African Litera-
       ture. Edited by Ulli Beier. Evanston, Ill.: Northwestern
       University Press, 1967, pp. 167-78.

212 JERVIS, STEVEN. "Tradition and Change in Hardy and Achebe."
       Black Orpheus, 2, Nos. 5-6 (1970), 31-38.

Achebe, Chinua

213   JOHNSON, JOHN WILLIAM. "Folklore in Achebe's Novels." New
      Letters, 40, No. 3 (Spring 1974), 95-107.
          Analyzes forms of folklore other than the proverb and
      the folktale.

214   JONES, RHONDA. "Art and Social Responsibility: Two Paths to
      Commitment." Ufahamu, 6, No. 2 (1976), 119-31.
          Examines Achebe and Ezekiel Mphahlele, a South African.

215   KEMOLI, ARTHUR M. "The Novels of Achebe: A Prophecy of
      Violence." Joliso, 2, No. 1 (1974), 47-66.
          Concentrates on Things Fall Apart and Arrow of God.

216   KILLAM, GORDON DOUGLAS. "Chinua Achebe's Novels." The
      Sewanee Review, 79, No. 4 (Autumn 1971), 514-41.

217   KILLAM, GORDON DOUGLAS. "Notes on Adaptation and Variation in
      the Use of English in Writing by Haliburton, Furphy, Achebe,
      Narayan and Naipaul." In The Commonwealth Writer Overseas:
      Themes of Exile and Expatriation. Edited by Alastair
      Niven. Brussels: Didier, 1976, pp. 121-35.

218   KILLAM, GORDON DOUGLAS. The Novels of Chinua Achebe. New
      York: Africana, 1969. 106 pp.

219   KLÍMA, VLADIMÍR. "Chinua Achebe's Novels." Philologica
      Pragensia, 12 (1969), 32-34.

220   LARSON, CHARLES R. "Characters and Modes of Characterization:
      Chinua Achebe, James Ngugi, and Peter Abrahams." In his
      The Emergence of African Fiction. Bloomington: Indiana
      University Press, 1971, pp. 147-66.

221   LAURENCE, MARGARET. "The Thickets of Our Separateness." In
      her Long Drums and Cannons. New York: Praeger, 1969,
      pp. 97-125.
          Interpretative analysis of his works.

222   LAWSON, WILLIAM. "Chinua Achebe in New England: An Inter-
      view." Yardbird Reader, 4 (1975), 99-110.

223   LESLIE, OMOLARA. "Chinua Achebe: His Vision and His Craft."
      Black Orpheus, 2, No. 7 (1971-1972), 34-41.

224   LESLIE, OMOLARA. "Nigeria, Alienation and the Novels of
      Achebe." Présence Africaine, No. 84 (1972), pp. 99-108.
      Reprinted in Black World, 22, No. 8 (June 1973), 34-43.
          The effects of colonialism in Achebe's novels.

Achebe, Chinua

225   LINDFORS, BERNTH. "Achebe on Commitment and African Writers."
       Africa Report, 15, No. 3 (March 1970), 16-18.
       Interview.

226   LINDFORS, BERNTH. "Chinua Achebe: An Interview." Studies in
       Black Literature, 2, No. 1 (Spring 1971), 1-5.

227   LINDFORS, BERNTH. "Chinua Achebe and the Nigerian Novel." In
       Studies on Modern Black African Literature. Edited by Pál
       Páricsy. Studies on Developing Countries, No. 43.
       Budapest: Hungarian Academy of Sciences Center for Afro-
       Asian Research, 1971, pp. 29-47. Reprinted in Lotus:
       Afro-Asian Writings, No. 15 (January 1973), pp. 34-51.

228   LINDFORS, BERNTH. "Chinua Achebe's Proverbs." Nigerian
       Field, 35, No. 4 (October 1970), 180-85; 36, No. 1
       (January 1971), 45-48; 36, No. 2 (April 1971), 90-96; 36,
       No. 3 (July 1971), 139-43.
           An annotated list of all proverbs in Achebe's four
       novels.

229   LINDFORS, BERNTH. "Oral Tradition and the Individual Literary
       Talent." Studies in the Novel, 4, No. 2 (Summer 1972),
       200-17. Reprinted in his Folklore in Nigerian Literature.
       New York: Africana, 1973, pp. 23-50.
           Combining of traditional and modern elements in the
       works of Tutuola, Nzekwu, and Achebe.

230   LINDFORS, BERNTH. "The Palm Oil with Which Achebe's Words Are
       Eaten." African Literature Today, No. 1 (1968), pp. 3-18.
       Reprinted in his Folklore in Nigerian Literature. New
       York: Africana, 1973, pp. 73-93.
           Examines Achebe's use of the English language, focusing
       on the use of proverbs in Achebe's four novels.

231   LYNCH, BARBARA SUE. "The Collision of Cultures in the Novels
       of Miguel Angel Asturias, Jacques-Stephen Alexis and Chinua
       Achebe." Dissertation, University of Illinois at Urbana-
       Champaign, 1973.

232   MADUBUIKE, IHECHUKWU. "Achebe's Ideas on African Literature."
       New Letters, 40, No. 4 (Summer 1974), 79-91. Reprinted as
       "Achebe's Ideas on Literature." Black World, 24, No. 2
       (December 1974), 60-70. Reprinted as "Chinua Achebe: His
       Ideas on African Literature." Présence Africaine, No. 93
       (1975), pp. 140-52. Reprinted as "Chinua Achebe's Perspec-
       tive." Renaissance 2, No. 4 (1975), pp. 14-19.
           Achebe's concerns about Africa's past, use of a foreign
       language, and a writer's responsibilities as revealed in
       his novels.

26

233   MADUKA, CHUKWUDI THOMAS. "Politics and the Intellectual Hero:
        Achebe, Abrahams, Flaubert and Wright." Dissertation,
        University of Iowa, 1976.

234   MAZRUI, M. "Aspects of the Relationship between Individual
        and Society in Some African Fiction with Special Reference
        to the Works of Chinua Achebe and James Ngugi." Thesis,
        Makerere University, 1972.

235   McCARTNEY, BARNEY CHARLES. "The Traditional Satiric Method
        and Matter of Wole Soyinka and Chinua Achebe." Disserta-
        tion, University of Texas at Austin, 1976.

236   McDANIEL, RICHARD BRYAN. "The Python Episodes in Achebe's
        Novels." International Fiction Review, 3 (1976), 100-06.

237   McDANIEL, RICHARD BRYAN. "Stylistic Devices in the Narrative
        and Dialogue of Chinua Achebe's Prose." Thesis, University
        of New Brunswick, 1970.

238   McDOWELL, ROBERT. "Of What Is Past, Or Passing, Or to Come."
        Studies in Black Literature, 2, No. 1 (Spring 1971), 9-13.
            Achebe's ability to convey a feeling for the breakdown
        of a civilization.

239   MELONE, THOMAS. "Architecture du monde: Chinua Achebe et
        W. B. Yeats." The Conch, 2, No. 1 (March 1970), 44-52.

240   MELONE, THOMAS. Chinua Achebe et la tragédie de l'histoire.
        Dissertation, University of Grenoble, 1969. Paris:
        Présence Africaine, 1973. 310 pp.

241   MEZU, S. OKECHUKWU. "Littérature biafraise: Le tragique
        héros de Chinua Achebe." L'Afrique Littéraire et
        Artistique, No. 4 (April 1969), pp. 22-25.

242   MEZU, S. OKECHUKWU. "The Tropical Dawn: Chinua Achebe."
        Nigerian Students Voice, 2, No. 2 (January 1965), 2-6.

243   MOORE, GERALD. "Chinua Achebe: Nostalgia and Realism." In
        his Seven African Writers. London: Oxford University
        Press, 1962, pp. 58-72.

244   MORELL, KAREN L., ed. In Person: Achebe, Awoonor, and
        Soyinka at the University of Washington. Seattle:
        Institute for Comparative & Foreign Area Studies, Univer-
        sity of Washington, 1975.
            Lecture by Achebe, "Africa and Her Writers," discussion,
        and interview.

Achebe, Chinua

245   NANCE, CAROLYN. "Cosmology in the Novels of Chinua Achebe."
      The Conch, 3, No. 2 (September 1971), 121-36.
          Shows that the changing world view of the Igbo is dealt
      with in Achebe's four novels.

246   NKOSI, LEWIS. "Chinua Achebe." In African Writers Talking.
      Edited by Cosmo Pieterse and Dennis Duerden. New York:
      Africana, 1972, pp. 3-6.
          Interview.

247   NWOGA, DONATUS. "The Chi Offended." Transition, 4, No. 15
      (July-August 1964), 5.
          Letter which responds to Shelton's article. [263]

248   NWOGA, DONATUS. "Chinua Achebe." In African Writers Talking.
      Edited by Cosmo Pieterse and Dennis Duerden. New York:
      Africana, 1972, pp. 6-9.
          Interview.

249   OGUNGBESAN, KOLAWOLE. "Politics and the African Writer: The
      Example of Chinua Achebe." African Studies Review, 17,
      No. 1 (April 1974), 43-53.
          Achebe's attitude toward political commitment and its
      effect on his writing.

250   OKAFOR, RAYMOND NNADOZIE. "Alienation in the Novels of Chinua
      Achebe." Annales de l'Université d'Abidjan, 6D (1973),
      329-41.

251   OKAFOR, RAYMOND NNADOZIE. "Individual and Society in Chinua
      Achebe's Novels." Annales de l'Université d'Abidjan, 5D
      (1972), 219-43.
          Alienation of the Ibo, on the individual and the collec-
      tive levels, as a theme in Achebe's four novels.

252   OLNEY, JAMES. "The African Novel in Transition: Chinua
      Achebe." South Atlantic Quarterly, 70, No. 3 (Summer
      1971), 299-316.
          Things Fall Apart, No Longer at Ease, and A Man of the
      People as representations of a movement in the African
      novel from "tribal" concerns to the individual coping with
      a dual society.

253   PONNUTHURAI, CHARLES SARVAN. "The Pessimism of Chinua
      Achebe." Critique, 15, No. 3 (1972), 95-109.
          Pessimistic themes and plots in Achebe's four novels.

254   POVEY, JOHN. "The Novels of Chinua Achebe." In Introduction
      to Nigerian Literature. Edited by Bruce King. New York:
      Africana, 1972, pp. 97-112.

255   RAVENSCROFT, ARTHUR. Chinua Achebe. London: Longmans,
      Green, 1969. 40 pp.

256   "A Relevant Art: Paddy Kitchen Talks to Chinua Achebe."
      Times Educational Supplement (14 April 1972), p. 19.
      Interview.

257   SEITEL, PETER. "Proverbs: A Social Use of Metaphor." Genre,
      2, No. 2 (June 1969), 143–61.
      Uses examples from Achebe's novels.

258   SERUMAGA, ROBERT. "Chinua Achebe." In African Writers Talk-
      ing. Edited by Cosmo Pieterse and Dennis Duerden. New
      York: Africana, 1972, pp. 11–17.
      Interview.

259   SERUMAGA, ROBERT. "Chinua Achebe Interviewed." Cultural
      Events in Africa, No. 28 (March 1967), pp. i–iv.

260   SERUMAGA, ROBERT. "A Mirror of Integration." In Protest and
      Conflict in African Literature. Edited by Cosmo Pieterse
      and Donald Munro. New York: Africana, 1969, pp. 70–80.
      The integration of social experiences.

261   SEVERAC, ALAIN. "Chinua Achebe." Université de Dakar Annales
      de la Faculté des Lettres et Sciences Humaines, No. 2
      (1972), pp. 55–66.
      Biography and bibliography.

262   SHELTON, AUSTIN J. "Failures and Individualism in Achebe's
      Stories." Studies in Black Literature, 2, No. 1 (Spring
      1971), 5–9.
      Achebe's concern with "losers" in his novels vs. his
      statements about a need to celebrate his ancestral past.

263   SHELTON, AUSTIN J. "The Offended Chi in Achebe's Novels."
      Transition, 3, No. 13 (March/April 1964), 36–37.
      Proposes that an offended chi caused downfall of charac-
      ters in the Okonkwo family.

264   SHELTON, AUSTIN J. "The 'Palm-Oil' of Language: Proverbs in
      Chinua Achebe's Novels." Modern Language Quarterly, 30,
      No. 1 (March 1969), 86–111.

265   SIBLEY, FRANCIS M. "Tragedy in the Novels of Chinua Achebe."
      Southern Humanities Review, 9, No. 4 (Fall 1975), 359–73.

266   SILVER, HELENE. "Chinua Achebe; Biography." Africana Library
      Journal, 1, No. 1 (Spring 1970), 18–22.

Achebe, Chinua

267   SOILE, 'SOLA.   "The Myth of the Archetypal Hero in Two African
        Novelists: Chinua Achebe and James Ngugi."   Dissertation,
        Duke University, 1973.

268   SWADOS, HARVEY.   "Chinua Achebe and the Writers of Biafra."
        Sarah Lawrence Journal (Spring 1970), pp. 55-62.   Re-
        printed in New Letters, 40, No. 1 (Autumn 1973), 5-13.
        Achebe's activities during the war.

269   TAIWO, OLADELE.   "Chinua Achebe."   In his Culture and the
        Nigerian Novel.   New York: St. Martin's Press, 1976,
        pp. 111-48.

270   TIBBLE, ANNE.   "Chinua Achebe."   In her African English Lit-
        erature: A Short Survey and Anthology of Prose and Poetry
        up to 1965.   London: Peter Owen, 1965, pp. 101-11.   Re-
        printed in Modern Black Novelists: A Collection of Criti-
        cal Essays.   Edited by Michael G. Cooke.   Englewood Cliffs,
        N.J.:   Prentice-Hall, 1971, pp. 122-31.

271   TUCKER, MARTIN.   "Three West African Novelists."   Africa
        Today, 12, No. 9 (November 1965), 10-14.
            Discusses the themes in the novels of Tutuola, Ekwensi,
        and Achebe.

272   TURKINGTON, KATE.   "'This No Be Them Country':   Chinua
        Achebe's Novels."   English Studies in Africa, 14, No. 2
        (September 1971), 205-14.

273   UHIARA, ALBERT ONYENAULOYA.   "Two Dispensations: A Study of
        the Impact of Western Culture on Modern Nigeria as Re-
        vealed in the Novels of Chinua Achebe."   Thesis, City Uni-
        versity of New York (Queens), 1965.

274   VAVILOV, V. N.   "The Books of Nigerian Author Chinua Achebe."
        In Africa in Soviet Studies: Annual 1969.   Translated by
        R. F. Kostiyuk and V. A. Epshtein.   Moscow: Nauka, 1971,
        pp. 145-61.

275   VINCENT, THEO.   "Register in Achebe."   Journal of the Nigeria
        English Studies Association, 6, No. 1 (May 1974), 95-106.
            The variations of English language in Things Fall Apart
        and No Longer at Ease.

276   WALSH, WILLIAM A.   "Chinua Achebe."   In his A Manifold Voice:
        Studies in Commonwealth Literature.   New York: Barnes &
        Noble, 1970, pp. 48-61.

Achebe, Chinua

277   WALTERS, JUSTINE QUAGLIANO. "Igbo Aphorisms in the Novels of
         Chinua Achebe." Thesis, University of California,
         Berkeley, 1967.

278   WANJALA, CHRIS L. "Achebe: Teacher and Satirist." In his
         Standpoints on African Literature: Critical Essays.
         Nairobi: East African Literature Bureau, 1973, pp. 161-71.

279   West Africa, No. 2855 (3 March 1972), p. 249.
         Achebe's literary activities during and since the war
         in Nigeria.

280   WILLIAMS, PHILLIP G. "A Comparative Approach to Afro-American
         and Neo-African Novels: Ellison and Achebe." Studies in
         Black Literature, 7, No. 1 (Winter 1976), 15-18.

281   WRIGHT, ROBIN. "Achebe Writes about Developing Nigeria the
         Way Faulkner Did about the South." Christian Science
         Monitor, 26 December 1974, p. 9. Reprinted in Black Times,
         5, No. 9 (September 1975), 11.
         Achebe's development and ideas.

ARROW OF GOD--Reviews

282   ADAMS, PHOEBE. Atlantic Monthly, 220, No. 6 (December 1967),
         150.

283   ANIEBO, I. N. C. "Unsentimental Looks." Nigeria Magazine,
         No. 81 (June 1964), pp. 149-50.

284   Booklist, 64, No. 14 (15 March 1968), 824.

285   CHRIST, RONALD. New York Times Book Review, 72 (17 December
         1967), 22.

286   COLLIER, CARMEN P. Best Sellers, 27, No. 18 (15 December
         1967), 365-66.

287   ENRIGHT, D. J. New Statesman, 67, No. 1725 (3 April 1964),
         531.

288   FLAD, HARVEY K. Library Journal, 93, No. 3 (1 February 1968),
         569.

289   GINGER, JOHN. Black Orpheus, No. 16 (October 1964), pp. 59-60.

290   IRELE, ABIOLA. Présence Africaine, No. 52 (1964), pp. 235-38.
         Présence Africaine, English ed., 24 (1964), 234-37.

Achebe, Chinua

291 JONES, ELDRED. "Achebe's Third Novel." Journal of Common-
      wealth Literature, No. 1 (September 1965), pp. 176-78.

292 Kirkus Reviews, 35, No. 19 (1 October 1967), 1229.

293 MACKAY, MERCEDES. African Affairs, 63, No. 253 (October
      1964), 303-304.

294 MILLER, CHARLES. "Mixed Allegiances." Saturday Review, 51,
      No. 1 (6 January 1968), 30-31.

295 MOORE, GERALD. "Achebe's New Novel." Transition, 4, No. 14
      (May/June 1964), 52.

296 Publishers Weekly, 192, No. 14 (2 October 1967), 49.

297 REDDING, SAUNDERS. "Achebe's New Novel." African Forum, 1,
      No. 1 (Summer 1965), 142-43.

298 SCHMIDT, NANCY J. Africa Report, 9, No. 11 (December 1964),
      35-36.

299 Time, 90 (10 November 1967), E12, 114.

300 Times Literary Supplement (26 March 1964), p. 249.

301 TUCKER, MARTIN. Commonweal, 87, No. 9 (1 December 1967), 316.

302 ULASI, JAMES ADAORA. "Nigerian Relish." Central African
      Examiner, 7, No. 12 (June 1964), 11.

303 WREN, BOB. Afriscope, 5, No. 9 (September 1975), 43-44.

ARROW OF GOD--Criticism

304 BIČANIČ, SONIA. "Three Circles of Reality in Chinua Achebe's
      Arrow of God." Studia Romanica et Anglica, 33-36
      (1972-73), 251-64.

305 BOAFO, Y. S. KANTANKA. "Arrow of God: A Case Study of Meg-
      alomania." Asemka, 1, No. 2 (December 1974), 16-24.
      A study of the character Ezeulu.

306 EMENYONU, ERNEST. "Ezeulu: The Night Mask Caught Abroad by
      Day." Pan-African Journal, 4, No. 4 (Fall 1971), 407-19.

307   GERE, ANNE RUGGLES. "An Approach to Achebe's Fiction."
      Africa Quarterly, 16, No. 2 (October 1976), 27-35.
         Examination of the oratory of village meetings which
      give insight into the novel as a whole.

308   GLEASON, JUDITH. "Out of the Irony of Words." Transition,
      4, No. 18 (1965), 34-38.

309   JORDAN, JOHN O. "Culture Conflict and Social Change in
      Achebe's Arrow of God." Critique, 13, No. 1 (1971),
      pp. 66-82.

310   KILLAM, G. D. "Notions of Religion, Alienation and Archetype
      in Arrow of God." In Exile and Tradition: Studies in
      African and Caribbean Literature. Edited by Rowland Smith.
      New York: Africana, 1976, pp. 152-65.

311   KILLAM, G. D. "Recent African Fiction." Bulletin of the
      Association for African Literature in English, No. 1
      (1964?), pp. 1-10.

312   LEWIS, MARY ELLEN. "Beyond Content in the Analysis of Folk-
      lore in Literature: Chinua Achebe's Arrow of God."
      Research in African Literatures, 7, No. 1 (Spring 1976),
      44-52.

313   LEWIS, MAUREEN WARNER. "Ezeulu and His God." Black World,
      24, No. 2 (December 1974), 71-87.

314   LEWIS, MAUREEN WARNER. "Priest of a Dead God." African Stud-
      ies Association of the West Indies Bulletin, No. 7
      (December 1974), pp. 39-53.

315   LINDFORS, BERNTH. "Ambiguity and Intention in Arrow of God."
      Ba Shiru, 5, No. 1 (Fall 1973), 43-48.
         A study of the enigmatic character, Ezeulu.

316   LINDFORS, BERNTH. "The Folktale as Paradigm in Chinua
      Achebe's Arrow of God." African Studies Association annual
      meeting paper, 1969. Studies in Black Literature, 1, No. 1
      (Spring 1970), 1-15. Reprinted in his Folklore in Nigerian
      Literature. New York: Africana, 1973, pp. 94-104.

317   MELAMU, M. J. "The Quest for Power in Achebe's Arrow of God."
      English Studies in Africa, 14, No. 2 (September 1971),
      225-40.

Achebe, Chinua

318   NIVEN, ALASTAIR. "Another Look at Arrow of God." The Liter-
       ary Half-Yearly, 16, No. 2 (July 1975), 53-68.
          Discusses the revised edition of Arrow of God and pro-
       vides a general analysis.

319   OBIECHINA, EMMANUEL. "Culture Contact and Culture Conflict."
       In his Culture, Tradition and Society in the West African
       Novel. New York: Cambridge University Press, 1975,
       pp. 201-59.

320   OKAFOR, CLEM ABIAZIEM. "The Inscrutability of the Gods:
       Motivation of Behaviour in Chinua Achebe's Arrow of God."
       Présence Africaine, No. 63 (1967), pp. 207-14.

321   OKO, EMELIA ASEME. "The Historical Novel of Africa: A Socio-
       logical Approach to Achebe's Things Fall Apart and Arrow of
       God." The Conch, 6, Nos. 1-2 (1974), 15-46.

322   SOILE, 'SOLA. "Tragic Paradox in Achebe's Arrow of God."
       Phylon, 37, No. 3 (Fall 1976), 283-95.

323   SPENCE, JAMES A. "Power in Achebe's Arrow of God." The
       University Review, 37, No. 2 (December 1970), 157-58.
         Ezeulu's quest for power.

324   WREN, ROBERT M. "Achebe's Revisions of Arrow of God."
       Research in African Literatures, 7, No. 1 (Spring 1976),
       53-58.
         Close comparison of the two editions.

BEWARE, SOUL BROTHER, AND OTHER POEMS--Reviews

325   CALDER, ANGUS. New Statesman, 84, No. 2177 (8 December 1972),
       866.

326   EGUDU, R. N. "Poetry as Catharsis." Ikorok, 1, No. 1
       (July 1971), 48-54.

327   JONES, ELDRED DUROSIMI. African Literature Today, No. 6
       (1973), pp. 181-82.

328   KATZ, BILL. Library Journal, 97, No. 12 (15 June 1972),
       2191.

329   NWOGA, DONATUS I. Okike, 1, No. 2 (December 1971), 37-40.

330   Times Literary Supplement (4 May 1973), p. 491.

Achebe, Chinua

BEWARE, SOUL BROTHER, AND OTHER POEMS--Criticism

331   ROGERS, PHILIP. "Chinua Achebe's Poems of Regeneration."
      Journal of Commonwealth Literature, 10, No. 3 (April 1976),
      1-9.

CHRISTMAS IN BIAFRA--Reviews

332   Choice, 10, No. 8 (October 1973), 1203.

333   Kirkus Reviews, 41, No. 1 (1 January 1973), 27.

334   MENKITI, IFEANYI A. Library Journal, 98, No. 9 (1 May 1973),
      1493.

335   OKWU, EDWARD C. Ufahamu, 4, No. 1 (Spring 1973), 162-68.

CHRISTMAS IN BIAFRA--Criticism

336   BRUCHAC, JOSEPH. "Achebe as Poet." New Letters, 40, No. 1
      (Autumn 1973), 23-31.

Civil Peace--Criticism

337   BURNESS, DONALD B. "Solipsism and Survival in Achebe's
      'Civil Peace' and 'Girls at War.'" Ba Shiru, No. 5 (1973),
      pp. 64-67.

GIRLS AT WAR AND OTHER STORIES--Reviews

338   ADAMS, PHOEBE. Atlantic Monthly, 231, No. 5 (May 1973), 123.

339   Booklist, 69, No. 17 (1 May 1973), 832.

340   BROYARD, ANATOLE. New York Times (14 March 1973), p. 41.

341   BURNS, JIM. New Statesman, 83 (3 March 1972), 285-86.

342   Choice, 10, No. 8 (October 1973), 1203-04.

343   JOHNSON, JUDY. Library Journal, 98, No. 13 (July 1973), 2198.

344   JONES, D. A. N. Listener, 87, No. 2244 (30 March 1972),
      426-27.

345   Kirkus Reviews, 41, No. 2 (15 January 1973), 75.

346   "The Literature of Civil War." Times Literary Supplement
      (3 March 1972), p. 247.

Achebe, Chinua

347   MENKITI, IFEANYI A.   Library Journal, 98, No. 9 (1 May 1973), 1507.

348   MERCIER, VIVIAN.   World, 2, No. 7 (27 March 1973), 57.

349   MUDRICK, MARVIN.   Hudson Review, 26, No. 3 (Autumn 1973), 554-55.

350   New Yorker, 49, No. 8 (14 April 1973), 155.

351   Publishers Weekly, 203, No. 7 (12 February 1973), 64.

352   Saturday Review of the Arts, 1, No. 4 (7 April 1973), 95.

353   VINCENT, THEO.   "The Post-War Achebe."   Nigeria Magazine, No. 113 (September 1974), pp. 65-67.

354   Virginia Quarterly Review, 49, No. 3 (Summer 1973), cx.

355   WAUGH, AUBERON.   Spectator, 228, No. 7498 (11 March 1972), 396-97.

356   YARDLEY, JONATHAN.   New York Times Book Review (13 May 1973), p. 36.

Girls at War--Criticism

357   BURNESS, DONALD B.   "Solipsism and Survival in Achebe's 'Civil Peace' and 'Girls at War.'"   Ba Shiru, No. 5 (1973), pp. 64-67.

A MAN OF THE PEOPLE--Reviews

358   ADAMS, PHOEBE.   Atlantic Monthly, 218, No. 3 (September 1966), 141.

359   "African Tragi-Comedy."   Insight, No. 13 (July-September 1966), pp. 30-31.

360   ALLSOP, KENNETH.   Spectator, 216, No. 7179 (28 January 1966), 113.

361   BECKINSALE, MONICA.   Books and Bookmen, 11, No. 5 (February 1966), 33.

362   BIMS, HAMILTON.   Negro Digest, 16, No. 3 (January 1967), 52, 93-94.

Criticism of Nigerian Authors

Achebe, Chinua

363   Booklist, 63, No. 4 (15 October 1966), 228.

364   BURGESS, ANTHONY. The Listener, 75, No. 1923 (3 February 1966), 181.

365   Choice, 4, No. 12 (February 1968), 1378.

367   DALE, JAMES. Canadian Forum, 47 (June 1967), 69–71.

368   DARNBOROUGH, ANNE. "Quartet." The New African, 7, No. 1 (March 1967), 10–11.

369   DATHORNE, O. R. Black Orpheus, No. 21 (April 1967), p. 61.

370   FLAD, HARVEY K. Library Journal, 91, No. 14 (August 1966), 3761.

371   FREMONT-SMITH, ELIOT. "What a Terrible Lot!" New York Times (10 August 1966), p. 39.

372   GEORGE, GERALD. "Behind a Murky Story, Some Light on African Trends." National Observer, 5, No. 33 (15 August 1966), 21.

373   GREEN, ROBERT. "Nigeria's New Man: Chinua Achebe." Nation, 202, No. 16 (18 April 1966), 465–66.

374   HAIRSTON, LOYLE. "A Sensitive, Human Novel." Freedomways, 7, No. 1 (Winter 1967), 80–82.

375   JONES, D. A. N. "Poor Innocent Victims." New Statesman, 71, No. 1820 (28 January 1966), 132–33.

376   JONES, ELDRED. "Locale and Universe--Three Nigerian Novels." The Journal of Commonwealth Literature, No. 3 (July 1967), pp. 127–31.

377   Kirkus Reviews, 34, No. 15 (1 August 1966), 780.

378   LERNER, ARTHUR. Books Abroad, 41, No. 1 (Winter 1967), 113.

379   MACKAY, MERCEDES. African Affairs, 66, No. 262 (January 1967), 81.

380   MALKIN, MARY ANN O'BRIAN. Antiquarian Bookman, 39 (15 May 1967), 1955.

381   MOODY, H. L. B. "Shrewd Foreknowledge or Prophetic Guess." Nigeria Magazine, No. 89 (June 1966), pp. 129–31.

Achebe, Chinua

382   "Odili's Progress." <u>Times Literary Supplement</u>
      (3 February 1966), p. 77.

383   OKPEWHO, ISIDORE. <u>The New African</u>, 5, No. 2 (March 1966),
      40.

384   OTTAH, NELSON. "A Witty Prophet of Revolution." <u>Drum</u>
      [Nigeria ed.] No. 186 (October 1966), [p. 39].

385   SHRAPNEL, NORMAN. <u>Manchester Guardian Weekly</u>, 94, No. 5
      (3 February 1966), 10.

386   STEPHENS, ALONZO J. <u>Negro History Bulletin</u>, 31, No. 3
      (March 1968), 21-22.

387   <u>Time</u>, 88 (19 August 1966), 80, 84.

388   W., D. "Things Falling Apart." <u>West Africa</u>, No. 2539
      (29 January 1966), p. 120.

389   WILSON, ANGUS. "Tragi-Comedy from Africa." <u>The Observer</u>
      (30 January 1966), p. 27.

A MAN OF THE PEOPLE--Criticism

390   ANOZIE, SUNDAY O. "The Problem of Communication in Two West
      African Novels." <u>The Conch</u>, 2, No. 1 (March 1970), 12-20.
         Compares Achebe and Okara in terms of themes, attitudes
      toward English, and English usage.

391   LINDFORS, BERNTH. "Achebe's African Parable." <u>Présence
      Africaine</u>, No. 66 (1968), pp. 130-36.
         The coup in the novel was meant to be an African para-
      ble, not a Nigerian prophecy.

392   NGUGI WA THIONG'O. "Chinua Achebe: A Man of the People."
      In his <u>Homecoming: Essays on African and Caribbean Litera-
      ture</u>. New York: Lawrence Hill, 1973, pp. 51-54.

393   NWOGA, D. IBE. "Alienation in Modern African Fiction." <u>The
      Muse</u>, No. 5 (May 1973), pp. 23-27.

394   OBIECHINA, EMMANUEL. "Post-Independence Disillusionment in
      Three African Novels." In <u>Neo-African Literature and Cul-
      ture: Essays in Memory of Janheinz Jahn</u>. Edited by Bernth
      Lindfors and Ulla Schild. Wiesbaden: Heymann, 1976,
      pp. 119-46.

395   OKPAKU, JOSEPH O. "A Novel for the People." Journal of the
      New African Literature and the Arts, No. 2 (Fall 1966),
      pp. 76-80.

396   PALMER, EUSTACE. "Chinua Achebe." In his An Introduction to
      the African Novel. New York: Africana, 1972, pp. 48-84.

397   RICHARD, RENE. "A Man of the People (C. Achebe) et Iska
      (C. Ekwensi)." Annales de l'Université d'Abidjan, 3D
      (1970), 67-68.
          Discusses the novels' view toward politics.

398   WREN, ROBERT M. "Anticipation of Civil Conflict in Nigerian
      Novels: Aluko and Achebe." Studies in Black Literature,
      1, No. 2 (Summer 1970), 21-32.

399   YANKSON, KOFI. "The Structural Role of 'Eat' in A Man of the
      People." English Department Workpapers, 1 (March 1971),
      38-42.
          Eating, figuratively and literally, provides a major
      theme.

400   YANKSON, KOFI. "The Use of Pidgin in No Longer at Ease and A
      Man of the People." Asemka, 1, No. 2 (December 1974),
      68-79.

NO LONGER AT EASE--Reviews

401   A., S. African Horizon, No. 2 (January 1961), p. 34.

402   ADAMS, PHOEBE. Atlantic Monthly, 207, No. 4 (April 1961),
      119.

403   ARAGBABALU, OMIDIJI. Black Orpheus, No. 8 (1960), pp. 51-52.

404   BROOKS, JEREMY. "Crying in the Wilderness." The Guardian
      (16 September 1960), p. 6.

405   BYAM, MILTON S. Library Journal, 86, No. 11 (1 June 1961),
      2118.

406   CALIRI, FORTUNATA. America, 105, No. 2 (8 April 1961),
      114-16.

407   COLEMAN, JOHN. "Beloved Bush." Spectator, 205, No. 6904
      (21 October 1960), 616-17.

408   ENE, J. CHUNWIKE. Ibadan, No. 11 (February 1961), pp. 42-43.

Achebe, Chinua

409   F., D. San Francisco Sunday Chronicle This World
          (9 July 1961), p. 26.

410   GREEN, ROBERT. The Nation, 201, No. 11 (11 October 1965),
          224-25.

411   GRUNWALD, BEVERLY. Saturday Review, 44, No. 23 (10 June 1961),
          23, 25.

412   HEALEY, ROBERT C. New York Herald Tribune Lively Arts & Book
          Review (30 April 1961), p. 28.

413   LERNER, ARTHUR. Books Abroad, 35, No. 3 (Summer 1961), 233.

414   LOMAX, LOUIS E. New Leader, 44, No. 21 (22 May 1961), 22.

415   MACKAY, MERCEDES. African Affairs, 60, No. 241 (October 1961),
          549.

416   MATSHIKIZA, TODD. Drum [Nigeria ed.], No. 145 (May 1963),
          p. 30.

417   MKAPA, BEN. Transition, 2, No. 3 (January 1962), 36.

418   Publishers Weekly, 196, No. 7 (18 August 1969), 75.

419   SENANU, KOJO. "A Rebel Manque." Universitas, 4, No. 5
          (March 1961), 153.

420   Times Literary Supplement (14 October 1960), p. 666.

421   Virginia Quarterly Review, 37, No. 4 (Autumn 1961), cxx.

422   WATERHOUSE, KEITH. New Statesman, 60, No. 1540 (17 September
          1960), 398.

NO LONGER AT EASE--Criticism

423   DJANGONE-BI, N'GUESSAN. "Obi Okonkwo ou l'intellectuel dé-
          semparé." Annales de l'Université d'Abidjan, 8D (1975),
          229-45.

424   HORTON, ROBIN. "Three Nigerian Novelists." Nigeria Magazine,
          No. 70 (September 1961), pp. 218-24.

425   MILLS, PETER. Notes on Chinua Achebe's No Longer at Ease.
          Nairobi: Heinemann Educational Books, 1976. 32 pp.

426   MPONDO, SIMON. "L'Univers existentiel de l'intellectuel afri-
      cain chez Chinua Achebe." Présence Africaine, No. 70
      (1969), pp. 172-80.

427   OKUNNUGA, YEMI. "The Tragic Conflict in Achebe's No Longer at
      Ease." Journal of the Nigeria English Studies Association,
      2, No. 2 (1968), 141-42.

428   PALMER, EUSTACE. "Chinua Achebe." In his An Introduction to
      the African Novel. New York: Africana, 1972, pp. 48-84.

429   RICHARD, RENE. "No Longer at Ease (C. Achebe) et People of
      the City (C. Ekwensi)." Annales de l'Université d'Abidjan,
      3D (1970), 47-48.
         Discusses the theme of both novels: conflicts brought
      about by a change to urban living.

430   RIDDY, FELICITY. "Language as a Theme in No Longer at Ease."
      The Journal of Commonwealth Literature, No. 9 (July 1970),
      pp. 38-47.

431   TAIWO, OLADELE. "Chinua Achebe: No Longer at Ease." In his
      An Introduction to West African Literature. New York:
      Humanities, 1967, pp. 134-51.

432   WALI, OBIAJUNWA. "The Individual and the Novel in Africa."
      Transition, 4, No. 18 (1965), 31-33.
         A study of character in Camara Laye's Radiance of the
      King, Achebe's No Longer at Ease, and Okara's The Voice.

433   WILSON, RODERICK. "Eliot and Achebe: An Analysis of Some
      Formal and Philosophical Qualities of No Longer at Ease."
      English Studies in Africa, 14, No. 2 (September 1971),
      215-23.

434   YANKSON, KOFI. "The Use of Pidgin in No Longer at Ease and
      A Man of the People." Asemka, 1, No. 2 (December 1974),
      68-79.

THINGS FALL APART--Reviews

435   ADALI-MORTTI, GEORMBEEYI. "A Nigerian Novel." Universitas,
      3, No. 6 (June 1959), 184-85. Reprinted in Black Orpheus,
      No. 6 (November 1959), pp. 48-50.

436   APPIAH, PEGGY. "A West African Novelist." West Africa,
      No. 2148 (14 June 1958), p. 565.

Achebe, Chinua

437 BYAM, MILTON S. Library Journal, 84, No. 6 (15 March 1959), 860.

438 DAVIS, HASSOLDT. Saturday Review, 42, No. 5 (31 January 1959), 18.

439 FONLON, BERNARD and PETER OGBONNAYA. Présence Africaine, No. 23 (December 1958–January 1959), pp. 135–38.

440 MACKAY, MERCEDES. African Affairs, 57, No. 228 (July 1958), 242–43.

441 MACLEAN, UNA. Odu, No. 7 (March 1959), pp. 45–46.

442 MACRAE, DONALD. Twentieth Century, 172, No. 1018 (Summer 1963), 128.

443 N'DIAYE, JEAN-PIERRE. Jeune Afrique, No. 541 (18 May 1971), pp. 59–61.

444 NZEKWU, ONUORA. "An African on Africans." Nigeria Magazine, No. 64 (March 1960), pp. 105, 107.

445 OBUMSELU, BEN. Ibadan, No. 5 (February 1959), pp. 37–38.

446 Publishers Weekly, 196, No. 7 (18 August 1969), 75.

447 SPEED, DIANA. Black Orpheus, No. 5 (May 1959), p. 52.

THINGS FALL APART--Criticism

448 ACKLEY, DONALD G. "The Male-Female Motif in Things Fall Apart." Studies in Black Literature, 5, No. 1 (Spring 1974), 1–6.

449 ADELUSI, O. Things Fall Apart: Notes. Ibadan: Onibonoje Press, 1966. 96 pp.

450 BOAFO, Y. S. KANTANKA. "Okonkwo, or the Triumph of Masculinity as a Determinant of the Fall of a Hero." Asemka, 1, No. 1 (January 1974), 7–15.

451 CARTEY, WILFRED. "The Falling Away." In his Whispers from a Continent: The Literature of Contemporary Black Africa. New York: Random House, 1969, pp. 96–105.

452 CHAMPION, ERNEST A. "The Story of a Man and His People: Chinua Achebe's Things Fall Apart." Negro American Literature Forum, 8, No. 4 (Winter 1974), 272–77.

453   DEDENUOLA, J. "The Structure of Achebe's Things Fall Apart."
       Nigeria Magazine, No. 103 (December 1969-February 1970),
       pp. 638-39.

454   EZUMA, BEN. Chinua Achebe's Things Fall Apart in Questions
       and Answers. Onitsha: Etudo Ltd., 1965. 35 pp. Re-
       printed as Questions and Answers on Things Fall Apart with
       List of Suggested Questions, Phrases and Difficult Words
       Fully Explained. Onitsha: Tabansi Printing Enterprises,
       no date. 42 pp.

455   HEYWOOD, CHRISTOPHER. "Surface and Symbol in Things Fall
       Apart." Journal of the Nigeria English Studies Associa-
       tion, No. 2 (November 1967), pp. 41-45.
          Similarities between Things Fall Apart and Edwardian
       novels.

456   IYASERE, SOLOMON O. "Narrative Techniques in Chinua Achebe's
       Things Fall Apart." New Letters, 40, No. 3 (Spring 1974),
       73-93.

457   JABBI, BU-BUAKEI. Achebe: Things Fall Apart (Notes).
       Freetown: Fourah Bay College Bookshop, 1974. 59 pp.

458   JABBI, BU-BUAKEI. "Fire and Transition in Things Fall Apart."
       Obsidian, 1, No. 3 (Winter 1975), 22-36.
          Shows how characterization, imagery, and symbolism help
       convey the theme of transition.

459   JONES, ELDRED D. "Academic Problems and Critical Techniques."
       In African Literature and the Universities. Edited by
       Gerald Moore. Ibadan: Ibadan University Press, 1965,
       pp. 89-95.

460   JONES, ELDRED. "Language and Theme in Things Fall Apart."
       Review of English Literature, 5, No. 4 (October 1964),
       39-43.

461   KEMOLI, ARTHUR. Notes on Chinua Achebe's Things Fall Apart.
       Nairobi: Heinemann Educational Books, 1975. 44 pp.

462   KRONENFELD, J. Z. "The 'Communalistic' African and the 'In-
       dividualistic' Westerner: Some Comments on Misleading
       Generalizations in Western Criticism of Soyinka and
       Achebe." Research in African Literatures, 6, No. 2 (Fall
       1975), 199-225. Reprinted in Critical Perspectives on
       Nigerian Literature. Edited by Bernth Lindfors.
       Washington, D.C.: Three Continents Press, 1976,
       pp. 247-70.

Achebe, Chinua

463   LANDRUM, ROGER L. "Chinua Achebe and the Aristotelian Concept
      of Tragedy." Black Academy Review, 1, No. 1 (Spring 1970),
      22-30.
          Demonstrates how Things Fall Apart follows the
      Aristotelian formula for tragedy, but in terms of Ibo
      events and setting.

464   LARSON, CHARLES R. "Chinua Achebe's Things Fall Apart: The
      Archetypal African Novel." In his The Emergence of African
      Fiction. Bloomington: Indiana University Press, 1971,
      pp. 27-65.

465   LEACH, JOSEPHINE. "A Study of Chinua Achebe's Things Fall
      Apart in Mid-America." English Journal, 60, No. 8
      (November 1971), 1052-56.
          Things Fall Apart in a suburban high school classroom.

466   MEYERS, JEFFREY. "Culture and History in Things Fall Apart."
      Critique, 11, No. 1 (1968), pp. 25-32.
          Portrayal of the advent of colonialism.

467   MOORE, GERALD. Things Fall Apart--Chinua Achebe. London:
      Heinemann Educational Books, 1974. 10 pp.

468   NNOLIM, CHARLES E. "Achebe's Things Fall Apart: An Igbo Na-
      tional Epic." Black Academy Review, 2, Nos. 1-2 (Spring-
      Summer 1971), 55-60. Reprinted in Modern Black Literature.
      Edited by S. Okechukwu Mezu. Buffalo, N.Y.: Black Academy
      Press, 1971, pp. 55-60.
          Okonkwo as an epic hero.

469   OBIECHINA, EMMANUEL. "Culture Contact and Culture Conflict."
      In his Culture, Tradition and Society in the West African
      Novel. New York: Cambridge University Press, 1975,
      pp. 201-59.

470   OBIECHINA, EMMANUEL. "Structure and Significance in Achebe's
      Things Fall Apart." African Studies Association annual
      meeting paper, 1975. English in Africa, 2, No. 2 (Septem-
      ber 1975), 39-44.

471   OGUNMOLA, M. O. Study Notes on Chinua Achebe's Things Fall
      Apart. Oyo, Nigeria: Alliance West African Publ. & Co.
      Ltd., 1970. 41 pp.

472   OKO, EMELIA A. "The Historical Novel of Africa: A Sociologi-
      cal Approach to Achebe's Things Fall Apart and Arrow of
      God." The Conch, 6, Nos. 1-2 (1974), 15-46.

473 OSINOWO, O. <u>Notes on Things Fall Apart</u>. Ibadan: Progresso
     Publishers, 1970. 80 pp.

474 PALMER, EUSTACE. "Chinua Achebe." In his <u>An Introduction to
     the African Novel</u>. New York: Africana, 1972, pp. 48-84.

475 PRIEBE, RICHARD. "Fate and Divine Justice in <u>Things Fall
     Apart</u>." In <u>Neo-African Literature and Culture: Essays in
     Memory of Janheinz Jahn</u>. Edited by Bernth Lindfors and
     Ulla Schild. Weisbaden: Heymann, 1976, pp. 159-66.

476 RICE, MICHAEL. "<u>Things Fall Apart</u>: A Critical Appreciation."
     <u>CRUX</u>, 10, No. 2 (May 1976), 33-40.

476a RICHARD, RENE. "Le Monde s'effrondre (C. Achebe)." <u>Annales
     de l'Université d'Abidjan</u>, 3D (1970), 41-42.

477 SCHEUB, HAROLD. "When a Man Fails Alone." <u>Présence Africaine</u>,
     No. 74 (1970), pp. 61-89.
     A study of the character Okonkwo.

478 STOCK, A. G. "Yeats and Achebe." <u>The Journal of Commonwealth
     Literature</u>, No. 5 (July 1968), pp. 105-11.

479 WALI, OBIAJUNWA. "The Centre Holds." <u>Ibadan</u>, No. 7
     (November 1959), p. 6.
     Letter in response to review by Obumselu. [445]

480 WEINSTOCK, DONALD J. "Achebe's Christ Figure." <u>Journal of
     the New African Literature and the Arts</u>, Nos. 5-6 (Spring-
     Fall 1968), pp. 20-26.
     A study of the character Ikemefuna.

481 WEINSTOCK, DONALD J. "The Two Swarms of Locusts: Judgement
     by Indirection in <u>Things Fall Apart</u>." <u>Studies in Black
     Literature</u>, 2, No. 1 (Spring 1971), 14-19.

482 WEINSTOCK, DONALD J. and CATHY RAMADAN. "Symbolic Structure
     in <u>Things Fall Apart</u>." <u>Critique</u>, 11, No. 1 (1968),
     pp. 33-41.

CLEMENT AGUNWA

<u>MORE THAN ONCE</u>--Reviews

483 LARSON, CHARLES R. <u>Africa Report</u>, 12, No. 9 (December 1967),
     45-46.

Agunwa, Clement

484   LINDFORS, BERNTH. Books Abroad, 43, No. 1 (Winter 1969),
        155.

485   LINDFORS, BERNTH. "Nigerian Novels of 1967." Journal of New
        African Literature and the Arts, Nos. 13-14 (1972),
        pp. 71-72.

486   MALKIN, MARY ANN O'BRIAN. Antiquarian Bookman, 39
        (15 May 1967), 1955.

487   MUKURIA, ROSE. "A Story with a Deep Moral." Nexus, 2, No. 1
        (July 1968), 43-44.

488   PRICE, R. G. G. Punch, 252, No. 6605 (12 April 1967), 544.

489   Times Literary Supplement (20 April 1967), p. 325.

FRANK AIG-IMOUKHUEDE

490   MACLEAN, UNA. "Three One-Act Plays." Ibadan, No. 9 (June
        1960), p. 21.
          University College, Ibadan, performances of plays by
        Soyinka, Aig-Imoukhuede, and Esan.

YEMI AJIBADE

Parcel Post--Review of Production

491   NKOSI, LEWIS. "Theatre by Yemi Ajibade." Africa: Inter-
        national Business, Economic and Political Monthly, No. 57,
        (May 1976), p. 74.
          At Royal Court Theatre, London.

NTIEYONG UDO AKPAN

492   "Akpan at Enugu." West Africa, No. 2572 (17 September 1966),
        p. 1053.
          Biographical sketch.

Aluko, Timothy Mofolorunso

THE WOODEN GONG--Review

493   WRIGHT, EDGAR. Transition, 5, No. 25 (1966), 52-54.

TIMOTHY MOFOLORUNSO ALUKO

494   ADAMOLEKUN, 'LADIPO. "T. M. Aluko." Afriscope, 5, No. 2
      (February 1975), 57, 59.
         A review article of Aluko's novels.

495   BANJO, AYO. "Language in Aluko: The Use of Colloquialisms,
      Nigerianisms." Ba Shiru, 5, No. 1 (Fall 1973), 59-69.
         Considers dialogues between Yoruba speakers and English
      speakers.

496   GERE, ANNE RUGGLES. "West African Oratory and the Fiction of
      Chinua Achebe and T. M. Aluko." Dissertation, University
      of Michigan, 1974.

497   LINDFORS, BERNTH. "T. M. Aluko: Nigerian Satirist." African
      Literature Today, No. 5 (1971), pp. 41-53.
         Aluko's novels are examined individually.

498   NGUGI, JAMES. "Satire in Nigeria: Chinua Achebe, T. M.
      Aluko and Wole Soyinka." In Protest and Conflict in
      African Literature. Edited by Cosmo Pieterse and Donald
      Munro. New York: Africana, 1969, pp. 56-69. Reprinted
      in his [Ngugi wa Thiong'o] Homecoming: Essays on African
      and Caribbean Literature. New York: Lawrence Hill, 1973,
      pp. 55-66.
         Satire which serves to criticize social and political
      conditions in Nigeria.

499   OMOTOSO, KOLE. "Interview with T. M. Aluko." Afriscope, 3,
      No. 6 (June 1973), 51-52.
         Aluko discusses his lack of a moral stand in his novels.

500   PALMER, EUSTACE TAIWO. "Development and Change in the Novels
      of T. M. Aluko." World Literature Written in English, 15,
      No. 2 (1976), 278-96.
         Improvement of Aluko's style from One Man, One Wife to
      Kinsman and Foreman.

Aluko, Timothy Mofolorunso

501   TAIWO, OLADELE. "T. M. Aluko." In his <u>Culture and the</u>
       <u>Nigerian Novel</u>. New York: St. Martin's Press, 1976,
       pp. 149-80.

502   TAIWO, OLADELE. "T. M. Aluko: The Novelist and His Imagina-
       tion." <u>Présence Africaine</u>, No. 90 (1974), pp. 225-46.
       Shows how knowledge of the Yoruba and their varieties
       of English enhances Aluko's novels.

CHIEF, THE HONORABLE MINISTER--Reviews

503   ALLEN, PHILIP M. <u>Africa Report</u>, 16, No. 4 (April 1971), 41.

504   HURD, DOUGLAS. <u>Spectator</u>, 225, No. 7426 (24 October 1970),
       482.

505   MBENG, ALLAAJI. <u>Présence Africaine</u>, No. 86 (1973), pp. 195-96.

506   <u>Times Literary Supplement</u> (16 October 1970), p. 1184.

HIS WORSHIPFUL MAJESTY--Reviews

507   A., F. <u>West Africa</u>, No. 2919 (21 May 1973), p. 665.

508   PRIEBE, RICHARD. <u>Books Abroad</u>, 48, No. 2 (Spring 1974), 412.

KINSMAN AND FOREMAN--Reviews

509   AKINSOLA, ELIZABETH. <u>Nigeria Magazine</u>, No. 92 (March 1967),
       pp. 83-84.

510   ANOZIE, S. O. <u>Présence Africaine</u>, No. 62 (1967), pp. 202-03.

511   EDWARDS, ANNE-LOUISE. "Illuminating Examples." <u>The New</u>
       <u>African</u>, No. 51 [Vol. 7, No. 2] (1968), pp. 22-23.

512   LARSON, CHARLES R. <u>Africa Report</u>, 12, No. 9 (December 1967),
       45.

513   N., M. "The Day of Judgment." <u>West Africa</u>, No. 2603
       (22 April 1967), p. 529.

514   NAGENDA, JOHN. <u>Drum</u> [Nigeria ed.], No. 206 (June 1968).

515   <u>Times Literary Supplement</u> (20 April 1967), p. 325.

516   TUBE, HENRY. <u>Spectator</u>, 220, No. 7282 (19 January 1968), 73.

Aluko, Timothy Mofolorunso

KINSMAN AND FOREMAN--Criticism

517 STEGEMAN, B. "The Courtroom Clash in T. M. Aluko's Kinsman
     and Foreman." Critique, 17, No. 2 (1975), pp. 26-35.

ONE MAN, ONE MATCHET--Reviews

518 AMOSU, NUNASU. Black Orpheus, No. 19 (March 1966), p. 61.

519 ANIEBO, I. N. C. Nigeria Magazine, No. 85 (June 1965),
     pp. 141-44.

520 BURGESS, ANTHONY. Spectator, No. 7116 (13 November 1964),
     p. 643.

521 CASTON, GEOFFREY. "The African District Officer." African
     Forum, 1, No. 3 (Winter 1966), 124-25.

522 HUTCHINSON, ALFRED. "Quality and Less." New African, 4,
     No. 5 (July 1965), 114.

523 JONES, D. A. N. New Statesman, 69, No. 1768
     (29 January 1965), 164.

524 Times Literary Supplement (12 November 1964), p. 1016.

525 West Africa, No. 2517 (28 August 1965), p. 967.

526 WRIGHT, EDGAR. Transition, 5, No. 25 (1966), 52-54.

ONE MAN, ONE MATCHET--Criticism

527 WREN, ROBERT M. "Anticipation of Civil Conflict in Nigerian
     Novels: Aluko and Achebe." Studies in Black Literature,
     1, No. 2 (Summer 1970), 21-32.

ONE MAN, ONE WIFE--Reviews

528 Abbia, Nos. 17-18 (June-September 1967), pp. 200-01.

529 BEIER, ULLI. Black Orpheus, No. 6 (November 1959), pp. 52-54.

530 DIPOKO, MBELLA SONNE. Présence Africaine, No. 63 (1967),
     p. 263.

531 JABAVU, NONTANDO. "Life in Nigeria." West Africa, No. 2194
     (2 May 1959), p. 421.

Aluko, Timothy Mofolorunso

532   NZEKWU, ONUORA. "An African on Africans." <u>Nigeria Magazine</u>,
       No. 64 (March 1960), pp. 105, 107.

ELECHI AMADI

533   "Amadi's War Diary." <u>West Africa</u>, No. 2939 (8 October 1973),
       pp. 1421-22.
            Amadi talks about his literary activities and future
       plans.

534   FINCH, GEOFFREY J. "Tragic Design in the Novels of Elechi
       Amadi." <u>Critique</u>, 17, No. 2 (1975), pp. 5-16.

535   IVKER, BARRY. "Elechi Amadi: An African Writer between Two
       Worlds." <u>Phylon</u>, 33, No. 3 (Fall 1972), 290-93.
            In <u>The Concubine</u> and <u>The Great Ponds</u> Amadi shows his
       conflict between two worlds.

536   NIVEN, ALASTAIR. "The Achievement of Elechi Amadi." In
       <u>Common Wealth</u>. Edited by Anna Rutherford. Aarhus:
       Akademisk Boghandel, 1972, pp. 92-100.

537   TAIWO, OLADELE. "Onuora Nzekwu and Elechi Amadi." In his
       <u>Culture and the Nigerian Novel</u>. New York: St. Martin's
       Press, 1976, pp. 181-209.

THE CONCUBINE--Reviews

538   B., D. "Back to the Village." <u>West Africa</u>, No. 2558
       (11 June 1966), p. 657.

539   DARNBOROUGH, ANNE. "Quartet." <u>The New African</u>, 7, No. 1
       (March 1967), 10-11.

540   DIPOKO, MBELLA SONNE. <u>Présence Africaine</u>, No. 58 (1966),
       pp. 253-55. <u>Présence Africaine</u>, English ed., 30 (1966),
       248-49.

541   "How to Murder Your Husband." <u>Times Literary Supplement</u>
       (7 April 1966), p. 281.

542   JONES, ELDRED. "Locale and Universe--Three Nigerian Novels."
       <u>The Journal of Commonwealth Literature</u>, No. 3 (July 1967),
       pp. 127-31.

543   MAYNE, RICHARD. <u>New Statesman</u>, 71, No. 1827 (18 March 1966),
       388-89.

544 O'NEILL, MARGARET. Africa Report, 12, No. 1 (January 1967),
     61.

545 PALMER, EUSTACE. African Literature Today, No. 1 (1968),
     pp. 56-58.

546 THOMPSON, DAVID. New African, 5, No. 3 (April 1966), 73.

547 UBA, SAM. "A Classic Tragedy." Drum [Nigeria ed.], No. 187
     (November 1966).

548 UKA, KALU. Nigeria Magazine, No. 90 (September 1966),
     pp. 232-34.

549 VINCENT, THEO. Black Orpheus, No. 21 (April 1967), pp. 62-63.

THE CONCUBINE--Criticism

550 ASIKA, UKPARI A. West Africa, No. 2562 (9 July 1966), p. 771.
     A letter which responds to the review by D. B. [538]

551 NANDAKUMAR, PREMA. "Another Image of African Womanhood (An
     Appreciation of Elechi Amadi's The Concubine)." Africa
     Quarterly, 13, No. 1 (April-June 1973), 38-44.

552 NESBITT, RODNEY. Notes on Elechi Amadi's The Concubine.
     Nairobi: Heinemann Educational Books, 1976. 42 pp.

553 PALMER, EUSTACE. "Elechi Amadi." In his An Introduction to
     the African Novel. New York: Africana, 1972, pp. 117-28.

554 SCHEUB, HAROLD. "Two African Women." Revue des Langues Vi-
     vantes, 37, Nos. 5-6 (1971), 545-58, 664-81.
     A study of Nwapa's Efuru and Amadi's The Concubine.

THE GREAT PONDS--Reviews

555 C., M. Présence Africaine, No. 80 (1971), pp. 164-65.

556 Choice, 10, No. 8 (October 1973), 1204.

557 Kirkus Reviews, 41, No. 7 (1 April 1973), 405.

558 MORSBERGER, ROBERT E. Books Abroad, 44, No. 3 (Summer 1970),
     528.

559 Publishers Weekly, 203, No. 11 (12 March 1973), 61.

Amadi, Elechi

560   SEBUKIMA, DAVIS. *Mawazo*, 2, No. 3 (June 1970), 58-59.

561   SHERMAN, JACOB R. *Library Journal*, 98, No. 11 (1 June 1973), 1842.

562   TUBE, HENRY. *Spectator*, 223, No. 7369 (20 September 1969), 374.

563   UPDIKE, JOHN. *New Yorker*, 49, No. 48 (21 January 1974), 84-86, 89.

564   WORKMAN, J. W. *Black Orpheus*, 2, No. 4 (1970), 66-67.

SAMSON O. O. AMALI

SELECTED POEMS--Review

565   ARMSTRONG, R. G. "Selected Poems." *Ibadan*, No. 28 (July 1970), pp. 93-98.

SELECTED POEMS--Criticism

566   ARMSTRONG, R. G. "A Brief Rejoinder to McVeagh." *Ibadan*, No. 29 (July 1971), p. 100.

567   McVEAGH, JOHN. "The Last on Amali." *Ibadan*, No. 30 (1975), p. 42.
        Letter.

568   McVEAGH, JOHN. "Poetry and Mr. Amali." *Ibadan*, No. 29 (July 1971), pp. 93-97.
        Response to Armstrong's review. [565]

569   THOMSON, A. W. "The Last on Amali." *Ibadan*, No. 30 (1975), pp. 43-44.
        Letter.

I. N. C. ANIEBO

THE ANONYMITY OF SACRIFICE--Reviews

570   *Choice*, 13, No. 1 (March 1976), 78-79.

571   SINGH, KIRPAL. *Dhana*, 6, No. 1 (1976), 59-61.

52

Clark, John Pepper

572 THOMAS, PETER. <u>Books Abroad</u>, 49, No. 3 (Summer 1975), 596-97.

573 WRIGHT, BILLY. "Behind Biafran Lines." <u>Afriscope</u>, 4, No. 12 (December 1974), 51.

OLA BALOGUN

574 AKSELRAD, MADELEINE. "Ola Balogun." <u>L'Afrique Littéraire et Artistique</u>, No. 8 (December 1969), pp. 26-27.

575 "Propaganda and <u>Shango</u>." <u>West Africa</u> (5 December 1970), p. 1421.
     Biographical, with discussion of Balogun's play, <u>Shango</u>.

576 SAJOUX, THERESE. "Ola Balogun: Dramaturge d'une civilisation oubliée." <u>Bingo</u>, No. 221 (June 1971), pp. 30-31.
     Interview.

JOHN PEPPER CLARK

577 ADEMOLA, FRANCES. "J. P. Clark and His Audience." <u>African Forum</u>, 1, No. 2 (Fall 1965), 84-86.
     Because of difficult themes and techniques used in Clark's drama, his plays have not yet had a performance or an audience to do them justice.

578 EGUDU, ROMANUS NNAGBO. "The Matter and Manner of Modern West African Poetry in English: A Study of Okigbo, Clark, Awoonor-Williams and Peters." Dissertation, Michigan State University, 1966.

579 EZEOKOLI, VICTORIA CHINWENMA. "African Theatre--A Nigerian Prototype." Dissertation, Yale University, 1972.
     Form and language in the dramatic works of Clark and Soyinka.

580 FEARN, MARIANNE. "Modern Drama of Africa: Form and Content, A Study of Four Playwrights." Dissertation, Northwestern University, 1974.

581 FERGUSON, JOHN. "Nigerian Drama in English." <u>Modern Drama</u>, 11, No. 1 (May 1968), 10-28.
     Includes detailed discussion of the works of Clark and Soyinka.

Clark, John Pepper

582 GRAHAM-WHITE, ANTHONY. "The Plays of J. P. Clark and Wole
Soyinka." In his The Drama of Black Africa. New York:
Samuel French, 1974, pp. 117-45.

583 HADDAD, MARJORIE ARLENE. "Pollution and Purification in the
Novels and Plays of Wole Soyinka, Chinua Achebe, and John
Pepper Clark." Dissertation, New York University, 1976.

584 "Interview with John Pepper Clark." In Palaver: Interviews
with Five African Writers in Texas. Edited by Bernth
Lindfors et al. Austin: African & Afro-American Research
Institute, University of Texas, 1972, pp. 14-22.

585 IZEVBAYE, DAN. "The Poetry and Drama of John Pepper Clark."
In Introduction to Nigerian Literature. Edited by Bruce
King. New York: Africana, 1972, pp. 152-72.

586 JABBI, BU-BUAKEI. West African Poems (Fifteen Analyses).
Freetown: Fourah Bay Bookshop, 1974, pp. 8-21.
Analyzes "Ibadan," "Olokun," "Night Rain," "Fulani Cat-
tle," "Agbor Dancer," and "Abiku."

587 LAURENCE, MARGARET. "Rituals of Destiny." In her Long Drums
and Cannons: Nigerian Dramatists and Novelists. New York:
Praeger, 1969, pp. 77-96.
Interpretative analysis of his works.

588 McLOUGHLIN, T. O. "The Plays of John Pepper Clark." English
Studies in Africa, 18, No. 1 (March 1975), 31-40.

589 MOORE, GERALD. "Poetry and the Nigerian Crisis." Black
Orpheus, 2, No. 3 (1968), 10-13.
On Okigbo, Soyinka, and Clark.

590 NKOSI, LEWIS. "J. P. Clark." In African Writers Talking.
Edited by Cosmo Pieterse and Dennis Duerden. New York:
Africana, 1972, pp. 63-67.
Interview.

591 POVEY, JOHN F. "The Poetry of J. P. Clark: 'Two Hands a Man
Has.'" African Literature Today, No. 1 (1968), pp. 36-47.
Demonstrates how Clark's existence in two cultures is
reflected in his poetry.

592 RECKORD, BARRY. "Notes on Two Nigerian Playwrights." The New
African, 4, No. 7 (September 1965), 171.

Clark, John Pepper

593   SALKEY, ANDREW. "J. P. Clark." In African Writers Talking.
       Edited by Cosmo Pieterse and Dennis Duerden. New York:
       Africana, 1972, pp. 68-74.
           Interview.

594   SENKORO, F. E. M. K. "An Artist and His Society (The Trial of
       J. P. Clark)." Umma, 4, No. 2 (1974), 77-82.
           On Clark's poetry.

595   TAIWO, O. "Two Incantations to 'Abiku.'" Nigeria Magazine,
       No. 106 (September/November 1970), pp. 219-24.
           Compares poems entitled "Abiku" by Clark and Soyinka.
       Describes this Nigerian concept.

596   THOMSON, A. W. "The Political Occasion: A Note on the
       Poetry of John Pepper Clark." Journal of Commonwealth
       Literature, 7, No. 1 (June 1972), 83-91.

597   THUMBOO, EDWIN. "An Ibadan Dawn: The Poetry of J. P. Clark."
       Books Abroad, 44, No. 3 (Summer 1970), 387-92.

598   THUMBOO, EDWIN. "J. P. Clark--Two Seedlings and the Iroko."
       Mawazo, 1, No. 2 (December 1967), 70-72.
           Looks at the development of Clark's poetic style as
       shown in A Reed in the Tide and examines closely the poem,
       "Night Rain."

599   UDOEYOP, NYONG J. Three Nigerian Poets: A Critical Study of
       the Poetry of Soyinka, Clark and Okigbo. Ibadan: Ibadan
       University Press, 1973. 166 pp.

600   UYOVBUKERHI, ATIBOROKO. "Ritual in J. P. Clark's Drama."
       Ba Shiru, 7, No. 1 (1976), 34-43.

CASUALTIES: POEMS 1966-68--Reviews

601   BARRON, LOUIS. Library Journal, 96, No. 2 (15 January 1971),
       196.

602   Black World, 20, No. 4 (February 1971), 69.

603   CHEYNEY-COKER, SYL. "Visions and Reflections on War."
       Ufahamu, 1, No. 3 (Winter 1971), 93-98.

604   KERR, SUSAN ANDERSON. Books Abroad, 46, No. 1 (Winter 1972),
       171.

Criticism of Nigerian Authors

Clark, John Pepper

CASUALTIES: POEMS 1966-68--Criticism

605   BODUNRIN, A. "Politics in Poetry." African Statesman, 7,
      No. 1 (1972), 15-20.

The Masquerade--Reviews of Productions

606   BILLINGTON, MICHAEL. Plays and Players, 13, No. 2 (November
      1965), 34.
         London, performed by the Eastern Nigeria Theatre Group
         for the Commonwealth Arts Festival.

607   "A Fierce Code Dramatized." The Times (17 September 1965),
      p. 13.
         London, performed by the Eastern Nigeria Theatre Group
         for the Commonwealth Arts Festival.

608   GILLIATT, PENELOPE. "A Nigerian Original." The Observer
      (19 September 1965), p. 25.
         London, performed by the Eastern Nigeria Theatre Group
         for the Commonwealth Arts Festival.

609   M., J. A. "Clark and Soyinka at the Commonwealth Arts Festi-
      val." The New African, 4, No. 8 (October 1965), 195.
         London, performed by the Eastern Nigeria Theatre Group.

610   OLUSOLA, SEGUN. "Three Nights of J. P. Clark." Nigeria Maga-
      zine, No. 85 (June 1965), pp. 156-60.
         Theatre Workshop production.

OZIDI--Reviews

611   ARAGBABALU, OMIDIJI. Black Orpheus, No. 22 (August 1967),
      pp. 60-61.

612   BANHAM, MARTIN. Books Abroad, 42, No. 1 (Winter 1968), 170.

613   BANHAM, MARTIN. "Nigerian Dramatists." The Journal of Com-
      monwealth Literature, No. 7 (July 1969), pp. 132-36.

OZIDI--Criticism

614   AKYEA, E. OFORI. "Traditionalism in African Literature:
      J. P. Clark." In Perspectives on African Literature.
      Edited by Christopher Heywood. New York: Africana, 1971,
      pp. 117-25.

Clark, John Pepper

615   LARSON, CHARLES R. "Nigerian Drama Comes of Age." <u>Africa</u>
        <u>Report</u>, 13, No. 5 (May 1968), 55-57.
           Discusses Clark's <u>Ozidi</u> and Soyinka's <u>Kongi's Harvest</u> as
        evidence of a new age of Nigerian drama.

POEMS--Reviews

616   BANHAM, MARTIN. <u>Books Abroad</u>, 38, No. 1 (Winter 1964), 92.

617   BEIER, ULLI. "Three Mbari Poets." <u>Black Orpheus</u>, 12 (1963?),
        46-50.

618   CUTLER, BRUCE. <u>Prairie Schooner</u>, 38, No. 2 (Summer 1964),
        178-81.

619   WILLIAMS, DENIS. "The Mbari Publications." <u>Nigeria Magazine</u>,
        No. 75 (December 1962), p. 71.

POEMS--Criticism

620   ANOZIE, SUNDAY O. "Two Nigerian Poets." <u>African Writer</u>, 1,
        No. 1 (August 1962), 3-4, 26-28.

621   EGUDU, ROMANUS. "J. P. Clark as a Bastard Child: A Study of
        'Ivbie.'" <u>Journal of the New African Literature and the</u>
        <u>Arts</u>, Nos. 13-14 (1972), pp. 21-26.

622   NNOKA, BARBARA GRANT. "Authenticity in John Pepper Clark's
        Early Poems and Plays." <u>Literature East and West</u>, 12,
        No. 1 (March 1968), 56-67.
           Portrayal of the Niger River Delta region in Clark's
        <u>Poems</u> and <u>Three Plays</u>.

623   THEROUX, PAUL. "Voices Out of the Skull; A Study of Six
        African Poets." <u>Black Orpheus</u>, No. 20 (August 1966),
        pp. 41-58. Reprinted in <u>Introduction to African Litera-</u>
        <u>ture</u>. Edited by Ulli Beier. Evanston, Ill.: Northwestern
        University Press, 1967, pp. 110-31.

<u>The Raft</u>--Review of Production

624   OBUMSELU, BEN. <u>Ibadan</u>, No. 19 (June 1964), pp. 51-52.
           Premiere performance at the Arts Theatre, Ibadan, April
        1964.

Clark, John Pepper

The Raft--Criticism

625   EGUDU, R. N. "J. P. Clark's The Raft: The Tragedy of Eco-
       nomic Impotence." World Literature Written in English, 15,
       No. 2 (November 1976), 297-304.

A REED IN THE TIDE--Reviews

626   CAREY, JOHN. New Statesman, 70, No. 1816 (31 December 1965),
       1032-33.

627   DIPOKO, MBELLA SONNE. Présence Africaine, No. 58 (1966),
       pp. 258-59. Présence Africaine, English ed., 30 (1966),
       353-54.

628   DUNCAN, BERNICE G. Books Abroad, 40, No. 3 (Summer 1966),
       361.

629   IGWE, B. EZUMA. "Three African Poets: A Critical Review."
       Journal of the New African Literature and the Arts,
       Nos. 11-12 (1971), pp. 83-90.

630   IRELAND, KEVIN. "Place and Poetic Identity." The Journal of
       Commonwealth Literature, No. 2 (December 1966), pp. 157-60.

631   LIYONG, TABAN LO. "Two by J. P. Clark." African Forum, 2,
       No. 1 (Summer 1966), 110-13.

632   MARTIN, GRAHAM. The Listener, 75, No. 1928 (10 March 1966),
       359.

633   OLEGHE, P. E. Education, 1, No. 2 (December 1968), 25-27.

A REED IN THE TIDE--Criticism

634   WANJALA, C. L. "Poets with Borrowed Overcoats Can Still Re-
       tain Their Personality: A Brief Study of A Reed in the
       Tide by John Pepper Clark." Busara, 7, No. 1 (1975), 20-25.

SONG OF A GOAT--Reviews

635   CUTLER, BRUCE. Prairie Schooner, 38, No. 2 (Summer 1964),
       178-81.

636   JONES, LeROI. Poetry, 103, No. 6 (March 1964), 399-400.

637   KOLLVITZ, D. M. Quadrant, 7, No. 3 (Winter 1963), 83-84.

Clark, John Pepper

638   WILLIAMS, DENIS. "The Mbari Publications." Nigeria Magazine,
       No. 75 (December 1962), pp. 70-71.

SONG OF A GOAT--Reviews of Productions

639   BILLINGTON, MICHAEL. Plays and Players, 13, No. 2 (November
       1965), 34.
          London, performed by the Eastern Nigeria Theatre Group
          for the Commonwealth Arts Festival.

640   "A Fierce Code Dramatized." The Times (17 September 1965),
       p. 13.
          London, performed by the Eastern Nigeria Theatre Group
          for the Commonwealth Arts Festival.

641   GILLIATT, PENELOPE. "A Nigerian Original." The Observer
       (19 September 1965), p. 25.
          London, performed by the Eastern Nigeria Theatre Group
          for the Commonwealth Arts Festival.

642   M., J. A. "Clark and Soyinka at the Commonwealth Arts Festi-
       val." The New African, 4, No. 8 (October 1965), 195.
          London, performed by the Eastern Nigeria Theatre Group.

643   NWANKWO, NKEM. Nigeria Magazine, No. 72 (March 1962), p. 80.
          Ibadan, Mbari Club.

644   OLUSOLA, SEGUN. "Three Nights of J. P. Clark." Nigeria Maga-
       zine, No. 85 (June 1965), pp. 156-60.
          The Eastern Nigeria Theatre Group.

645   SPURLING, HILARY. The Spectator (24 September 1965), p. 380.
          London, performed by the Eastern Nigeria Theatre Group
          for the Commonwealth Arts Festival.

SONG OF A GOAT--Criticism

646   ADEDEJI, J. A. "Some Notes on Song of a Goat by J. P. Clark."
       Ibadan, No. 28 (July 1970), pp. 99-101.

647   ARMSTRONG, ROBERT G. Ibadan, No. 15 (March 1963), pp. 29-30.

648   MACLEAN, UNA. Ibadan, No. 14 (October 1962), pp. 28-29.

Clark, John Pepper

THREE PLAYS--Reviews

649   FITZGERALD, ROBERT. "J. P. Clark's Plays." African Forum,
       1, No. 1 (Summer 1965), 143-45.

650   HILL, GEOFFREY. "Nigerian Plays." The Journal of Common-
       wealth Literature, No. 1 (September 1965), pp. 172-74.

651   KENNARD, PETER. "Recent African Drama." Bulletin of the
       Association for African Literature in English, No. 1
       (1964?), pp. 11-18.

652   LARSON, CHARLES. Africa Report, 11, No. 8 (November 1966),
       57-58.

653   Times Literary Supplement (13 August 1964), p. 728.

THREE PLAYS--Criticism

654   ASTRACHAN, ANTHONY. "Like Goats to the Slaughter." Black
       Orpheus, No. 16 (October 1964), pp. 21-24.
       A close look at each play.

655   ESSLIN, MARTIN. "Two African Playwrights." Black Orpheus,
       No. 19 (March 1966), pp. 33-39. Reprinted in Introduction
       to African Literature. Edited by Ulli Beier. Evanston,
       Ill.: Northwestern University Press, 1967, pp. 255-62.

656   NNOKA, BARBARA GRANT. "Authenticity in John Pepper Clark's
       Early Poems and Plays." Literature East and West, 12,
       No. 1 (March 1968), 56-67.
       Portrayal of the Niger River Delta region in Clark's
       Poems and Three Plays.

MICHAEL J. C. ECHERUO

657   LINDFORS, BERNTH. "Interview with Michael Echeruo."
       Greenfield Review, 3, No. 4 (1974), 48-59. Reprinted in
       his Dem-Say: Interviews with Eight Nigerian Writers.
       Austin: African and Afro-American Studies and Research
       Center, University of Texas, 1974, pp. 5-15.

MORTALITY--Reviews

658   FALVEY, P. Journal of the Nigeria English Studies Association,
       3, No. 1 (1969), 139-40.

Egbuna, Obi

659   MAES-JELINEK, H. Revue des Langues Vivantes, 37, No. 4
       (1971), 491-92.

660   MOORE, GERALD. The Conch, 1, No. 2 (September 1969), 60-61.

661   MORSBERGER, ROBERT E. Books Abroad, 44, No. 3 (Summer 1970),
       528.

662   OKONKWO, JULIET I. The Muse, No. 4 (May 1972), pp. 36-38.

663   "Paths to Refinement." Times Literary Supplement
       (24 July 1969), p. 836.

664   RØNNING, HELGE. African Affairs, 68, No. 272 (July 1969),
       279.

MORTALITY--Criticism

665   CALDER, ANGUS. "A Sense of Shame." Busara, 2, No. 2 (1969),
       15-28. Reprinted in Standpoints on African Literature:
       Critical Essays. Edited by Chris L. Wanjala. Nairobi:
       East African Literature Bureau, 1973, pp. 264-83.
       Compares Echeruo, Christopher Okigbo, and Kwesi Brew.

OBI EGBUNA

666   LINDFORS, BERNTH. "Interview with Obi Egbuna." In his Dem-
       Say: Interviews with Eight Nigerian Writers." Austin:
       African and Afro-American Studies and Research Center,
       University of Texas, 1974, pp. 16-23.

667   NWIMO, EMMA. "My Name is Obi." Drum, No. 282 (October 1974).
       Interview.

The Agony--Review of Production

668   GRIOT. "Black Theatre." West Africa, No. 2751 (28 February
       1970), pp. 226-27.
       London, Unity Theatre.

THE ANTHILL--Reviews

669   BROWN, JOE CHUKWUEMEKA. West Africa, No. 2603 (22 April
       1967), pp. 529-30.

670   Choice, 4, No. 2 (April 1967), 179.

Egbuna, Obi

671   LINDFORS, BERNTH. Books Abroad, 40, No. 3 (Summer 1966),
      360.

THE ANTHILL--Criticism

672   RAMASWAMY, S. "A Well Made Nigerian Play." Literary Half-
      Yearly, 17, No. 2 (July 1976), 109-13.

EMPEROR OF THE SEA--Review

673   Afriscope, 4, No. 4 (April 1974), 48.

WIND VERSUS POLYGAMY--Reviews

674   DATHORNE, O. R. Black Orpheus, No. 17 (June 1965), p. 59.

675   DICK, KAY. Spectator (4 December 1964), p. 788.

676   No entry.

677   No entry.

678   DIPOKO, MBELLA SONNE. Présence Africaine, No. 53 (1965),
      pp. 276-78. Présence Africaine, English ed., 25 (1965),
      275-76.

679   JONES, D. A. N. New Statesman, 69, No. 1768 (29 January 1965),
      164.

680   MACMILLAN, M. The Journal of Commonwealth Literature, No. 1
      (September 1965), pp. 174-75.

681   POLLOCK, VENETIA. Punch, 248, No. 6488 (13 January 1965), 69.

682   Times Literary Supplement (10 December 1964), p. 1121.

683   W., K. West Africa, No. 2517 (28 August 1965), p. 967.

WIND VERSUS POLYGAMY--Criticism

684   TAIWO, OLADELE. "Social Criticism." In his Culture and the
      Nigerian Novel. New York: St. Martin's Press, 1976,
      pp. 34-73.

CYPRIAN EKWENSI

685 DATHORNE, O. R. "Cyprian Ekwensi: The African Novelist and
     the People." In Mélanges (reflexions d'hommes de culture).
     Paris: Présence Africaine, 1969, pp. 230-40.

686 DUERDEN, DENNIS. "Cyprian Ekwensi." In African Writers Talk-
     ing. Edited by Cosmo Pieterse and Dennis Duerden. New
     York: Africana, 1972, pp. 80-83.
     Interview.

687 ECHERUO, M. J. C. "The Fiction of Cyprian Ekwensi." Nigeria
     Magazine, No. 75 (December 1962), pp. 63-66.
     Points out weaknesses of Ekwensi's novels.

688 EKWENSI, CYPRIAN. "Literary Influences on a Young Nigerian."
     Times Literary Supplement (4 June 1964), pp. 475-76.
     English literature which influenced Ekwensi and a de-
     fense of the realism in his novels.

689 EMENYONU. ERNEST. Cyprian Ekwensi. London: Evans, 1974.
     137 pp.

690 "Entretien avec l'écrivain nigérien Cyprian Ekwensi."
     Afrique, No. 24 (May 1963), pp. 49-51.

691 GREENSTEIN, SUSAN M. "Cyprian Ekwensi and Onitsha Market
     Literature." In Essays in African Literature. Spectrum
     Monograph Series in the Arts and Sciences, 3. Edited by
     W. L. Ballard. Atlanta: School of Arts and Sciences,
     Georgia State University, 1973, pp. 175-91.

692 KILLAM, DOUGLAS. "Cyprian Ekwensi." In Introduction to
     Nigerian Literature. Edited by Bruce King. New York:
     Africana, 1972, pp. 77-96.

693 LAURENCE, MARGARET. "Masks of the City." In her Long Drums
     and Cannons: Nigerian Dramatists and Novelists. New York:
     Praeger, 1969, pp. 148-68.
     Interpretative analysis of his works.

694 LINDFORS, BERNTH. "The Blind Men and the Elephant." African
     Literature Today, No. 7 (1975), pp. 53-64.
     Critics of Nigerian literature (particularly Gareth
     Griffiths and Ernest Emenyonu) and attitudes toward non-
     African critics.

Ekwensi, Cyprian

695   LINDFORS, BERNTH. "Cyprian Ekwensi--An African Popular Nov-
        elist." African Literature Today, No. 3 (1969), pp. 2-14.
        Reprinted in his Folklore in Nigerian Literature. New York:
        Africana, 1973, pp. 116-29.
            The worst elements of Western popular literature com-
        bined with the least subtle techniques of African oral
        literature serve to make Ekwensi novels unsuccessful.
        Several works are discussed.

696   LINDFORS, BERNTH. "Interview with Cyprian Ekwensi." World
        Literature Written in English, 13, No. 2 (November 1974),
        141-54. Reprinted in his Dem-Say: Interviews with Eight
        Nigerian Writers. Austin: African and Afro-American
        Studies and Research Center, University of Texas, 1974,
        pp. 24-34.

697   McCLUSKY, JOHN. "The City as a Force: Three Novels by
        Cyprian Ekwensi." Journal of Black Studies, 7, No. 2
        (December 1976), 211-24.
            People of the City, Jagua Nana, and Beautiful Feathers.

698   McDOWELL, ROBERT E. "Three Nigerian Storytellers: Okara,
        Tutuola, and Ekwensi." Ball State University Forum, 10,
        No. 3 (Summer 1969), 67-75.
            The three authors' works have in common the influence of
        oral tradition and African characters without European
        contact.

699   NKOSI, LEWIS. "Cyprian Ekwensi." In African Writers Talking.
        Edited by Cosmo Pieterse and Dennis Duerden. New York:
        Africana, 1972, pp. 77-80.
            Interview.

700   OBIECHINA, E. N. "Ekwensi as Novelist." Présence Africaine,
        No. 86 (1973), pp. 152-64.
            Theme and technique in Ekwensi's novels.

701   OKONKWO, JULIET I. "Ekwensi and Modern Nigerian Culture."
        Ariel, 7, No. 2 (April 1976), 32-45.

702   PASSMORE, DENNIS R. "Camp Style in the Novels of Cyprian
        Ekwensi." Journal of Popular Culture, 4, No. 3 (Winter
        1971), 705-16.
            Shows how Ekwensi's artistic failures can be appreciated
        as a source of amusement.

Ekwensi, Cyprian

703 POVEY, JOHN. "Cyprian Ekwensi: The Novelist and the Pressure
     of the City." In The Critical Evaluation of African Liter-
     ature. Edited by Edgar Wright. Washington, D.C.:
     Inscape, 1976, pp. 73-94.

704 TUCKER, MARTIN. "Three West African Novelists." Africa
     Today, 12, No. 9 (November 1965), 10-14.
     Themes in the novels of Tutuola, Ekwensi, and Achebe.

705 West Africa, No. 2748 (31 January 1970), p. 137.
     Ekwensi's opinion about the civil war in Nigeria.

AN AFRICAN NIGHT'S ENTERTAINMENT--Review

706 Times Literary Supplement (20 September 1963), p. 709.

AN AFRICAN NIGHT'S ENTERTAINMENT--Criticism

707 SKINNER, NEIL. "From Hausa to English: A Study in Para-
     phrase." Research in African Literatures, 4, No. 2 (Fall
     1973), 154-64. Reprinted in Critical Perspectives on
     African Literatures. Edited by Bernth Lindfors.
     Washington, D.C.: Three Continents Press, 1976,
     pp. 147-58.
     An African Night's Entertainment is shown to be a para-
     phrased translation of a Hausa tale published earlier.

BEAUTIFUL FEATHERS--Reviews

708 ALLEN, WALTER. New Statesman, 65, No. 1679 (17 May 1963),
     754.

709 LIGNY, MICHEL. Présence Africaine, No. 51 (1964), pp. 181-82.
     Présence Africaine, English ed., 23 (1964), 177-78.

710 NAGENDA, JOHN. "Average Entertainment." New African, 2,
     No. 7 (17 August 1963), 137.

711 NICHOLSON, MARJORIE. African Affairs, 64, No. 256 (July
     1965), 224-25.

712 NICHOLSON, MARJORIE. African Affairs, 65, No. 258 (January
     1966), 100-01.

713 "Seeing Life in Lagos." Times Literary Supplement
     (17 May 1963), 353.

714 The Times Weekly Review (23 May 1963), p. 13.

Ekwensi, Cyprian

BEAUTIFUL FEATHERS--Criticism

715   POVEY, JOHN F. "Cyprian Ekwensi and Beautiful Feathers."
       Critique, 8, No. 1 (Fall 1965), 63-69.

716   SHELTON, AUSTIN JESSE. "Pan Africanism and Beautiful
       Feathers." Books Abroad, 39, No. 1 (Winter 1965), 34-36.
       Pan Africanism as a theme in Beautiful Feathers.

BURNING GRASS--Reviews

717   Books for Africa, 33, No. 2 (April 1963), 58-59.

718   PRYSE, B. ELIZABETH. "Getting into Perspective." Nigeria
       Magazine, No. 74 (September 1962), pp. 83-85.

719   Times Literary Supplement (7 September 1962), p. 669.

BURNING GRASS--Criticism

720   BONNEAU, DANIELLE. "Une Oeuvre méconnue de Cyprian Ekwensi:
       Burning Grass." Annales de l'Université d'Abidjan, 4D
       (1971), 5-30.

ISKA--Reviews

721   BIMS, HAMILTON, Negro Digest, 16, No. 2 (December 1966),
       68-69.

722   BYROM, BILL. Spectator, 217, No. 7209 (26 August 1966),
       264-65.

723   "A Cancerous Vitality." Times Literary Supplement
       (25 August 1966), p. 757.

724   MOODY, H. L. B. Nigeria Magazine, No. 103 (December 1969-
       February 1970), pp. 634-37.

725   W., D. "Ekwensi's Nigeria." West Africa, No. 2570
       (3 September 1966), p. 999.

ISKA--Criticism

726   RICHARD, RENE. "A Man of the People (C. Achebe) et Iska
       (C. Ekwensi)." Annales de l'Université d'Abidjan, 3D
       (1970), 67-68.
       The novels' view toward politics.

Ekwensi, Cyprian

JAGUA NANA--Reviews

727   BEIER, ULLI. Black Orpheus, No. 10 (1961), p. 68.

728   BERGONZI, BERNARD. Spectator, No. 6926 (24 March 1961),
       p. 416.

729   PRYCE-JONES, DAVID. Time and Tide, 42, No. 12 (23 March 1961),
       481.

730   Times Literary Supplement (31 March 1961), 197.

JAGUA NANA--Criticism

731   HORTON, ROBIN. "Three Nigerian Novelists." Nigeria Magazine,
       No. 70 (September 1961), pp. 218-24.

732   IDAPO, COZ. "Who's Afraid of Jagua Nana?" Drum [Nigeria
       ed.], No. 157 (May 1964).
           Discusses some Nigerians' criticism of the depiction of
       Nigerian life in Jagua Nana.

733   JULY, ROBERT W. "African Literature and the African Person-
       ality." Black Orpheus, No. 14 (February 1964), pp. 33-45.
       Reprinted in Introduction to African Literature. Edited by
       Ulli Beier. Evanston, Ill.: Northwestern University
       Press, 1967, pp. 218-33. Reprinted in Modern Black Novel-
       ists: A Collection of Critical Essays. Edited by Michael
       G. Cook. Englewood Cliffs, N.J.: Prentice-Hall, 1971,
       pp. 105-21.

734   SHELTON, AUSTIN J. "Le Principe cyclique de la personnalité
       africaine (II): 'Le retour à la brousse' ou le recul onto-
       logique." Présence Africaine, No. 46 (1963), pp. 64-77.
       "'Rebushing' or Ontological Recession to Africanism:
       Jagua's Return to the Village." Présence Africaine, En-
       glish ed., 18 (1963), 49-60.

LOKOTOWN AND OTHER STORIES--Reviews

735   LARSON, CHARLES R. Africa Report, 11, No. 7 (October 1966),
       75-76.

736   SCHMIDT, NANCY J. Journal of the New African Literature and
       the Arts, No. 2 (Fall 1966), pp. 71-73.

737   West Africa Link, 3, No. 6 (June 1966), 216.

Ekwensi, Cyprian

PEOPLE OF THE CITY--Reviews

738 BEVAN, ELIZABETH. Black Orpheus, No. 4 (October 1958),
pp. 53-55.

739 KWAPONG, A. A. "African Viewpoints." Universitas, 1, No. 5
(March 1955), 24-25.

740 MORGAN, WILLIAM. West African Review, 25, No. 327 (December
1954), 1217.

PEOPLE OF THE CITY--Criticism

741 NGANGA, BERNARD. "Tradition et modernisme dans People of the
City." Annales de l'Université de Brazzaville, 9 (1973),
49-54.

742 RICHARD, RENE. "No Longer at Ease (C. Achebe) et People of
the City." Annales de l'Université d'Abidjan, 3D (1970),
47-48.
On the theme of both novels: the conflicts brought
about by a change to urban living.

743 TAIWO, OLADELE. "Cyprian Ekwensi: People of the City." In
his An Introduction to West African Literature. London:
Nelson, 1967, pp. 152-62.

RESTLESS CITY AND CHRISTMAS GOLD--Review

744 Choice, 13, No. 8 (October 1976), 990.

BUCHI EMECHETA

745 "Two Faces of Emancipation." Africa Woman, No. 2 (December
1975-January 1976), pp. 47-49.
Biographical.

THE BRIDE PRICE--Reviews

746 Booklist, 72, No. 14 (15 March 1976), 1018.

747 Choice, 13, No. 7 (September 1976), 836.

748 CIMA, RICHARD. Library Journal, 101, No. 7 (1 April 1976),
922-23.

749 CLAPP, SUSANNAH. "An Ibo Girlhood." Times Literary Supplement (11 June 1976), p. 689.

750 CUNNINGHAM, VALENTINE. New Statesman, 91, No. 2362 (25 June 1976), 856.

751 Kirkus Reviews, 44, No. 3 (1 February 1976), 147.

752 New Yorker, 52, No. 13 (17 May 1976), 170-71.

753 OPPENHEIM, JANE. Best Sellers, 36 (July 1976), 108.

754 Publishers Weekly, 209, No. 8 (23 February 1976), 118.

755 ROBINSON, KATHRYN. School Library Journal, 23, No. 1 (September 1976), 143.

756 THWAITE, ANTHONY. "Faded Truths." Observer (20 June 1976), p. 27.

IN THE DITCH--Reviews

757 Observer (30 July 1972), p. 32.

758 "On the Welfare." Times Literary Supplement (11 August 1972), p. 936.

759 RAY, ROBERT. Books and Bookmen, 17, No. 12 (September 1972), 100.

SECOND-CLASS CITIZEN--Reviews

760 Booklist, 72, No. 7 (1 December 1975), 499.

761 Choice, 13, No. 1 (March 1976), 79.

762 JOHNSON, MARIGOLD. "Liberation Struggle." Times Literary Supplement (31 January 1975), p. 102.

763 Kirkus Reviews, 43, No. 13 (1 July 1975), 726.

764 LEVIN, MARTIN. New York Times Book Review (14 September 1975), p. 42.

765 Publishers Weekly, 207, No. 24 (16 June 1975), 74.

766 SIMMS, AURORA G. Library Journal, 100, No. 15 (1 September 1975), 1569-70.

Emecheta, Buchi

767   WALKER, ALICE. "A Writer Because of, Not in Spite of, Her
        Children." <u>Ms.</u>, 4, No. 7 (January 1976), 40.

768   WORDSWORTH, CHRISTOPHER. "A Bleak Version of Existence."
        <u>Guardian Weekly</u>, 112 (8 February 1975), p. 22.

YETUNDE ESAN

769   MACLEAN, UNA. "Three One-Act Plays." <u>Ibadan</u>, No. 9
        (June 1960), p. 21.
           University College, Ibadan, performances of plays by
        Soyinka, Aig-Imoukhuede, and Esan.

OYELEKE FOWOWE

<u>WHO HAS BLOOD?</u>--Review

770   LINDFORS, BERNTH. <u>Books Abroad</u>, 47, No. 3 (Summer 1973), 604.

RASHEED GBADAMOSI

<u>Behold My Redeemer</u>--Review of Production

771   <u>Afriscope</u>, 4, No. 3 (March 1974), 52.
           Lagos performance by Phoenix Playgroup.

<u>ECHOES FROM THE LAGOON</u>--Review

772   A., F. <u>West Africa</u>, No. 2970 (20 May 1974), p. 601.

<u>The Model Village</u>--Review of Production

773   OKONEDO, BOB. "African Theatre in London." <u>West Africa</u>,
        No. 2921 (4 June 1973), p. 741.
           Performance by Pan-African Theatre Company.

JAMES ENE HENSHAW

CHILDREN OF THE GODDESS AND OTHER PLAYS--Reviews

774   AXWORTHY, GEOFFREY. West African Journal of Education, 9,
      No. 2 (June 1965), 103, 105.

775   C., G. W. Eastern Nigeria School Libraries Association Bul-
      letin, 2, No. 1 (March 1966), 40.

776   KENNARD, PETER. "Recent African Drama." Bulletin of the
      Association for African Literature in English, No. 1
      (1964?), pp. 11-18.

MEDICINE FOR LOVE--Reviews

777   AXWORTHY, GEOFFREY. West African Journal of Education, 9,
      No. 2 (June 1965), 103, 105.

778   C., G. W. Eastern Nigeria School Libraries Association
      Bulletin, 2, No. 1 (March 1966), 40.

779   KENNARD, PETER. Bulletin of the Association for African Lit-
      erature in English, No. 2 (1964?), pp. 11-18.

780   OGUNDE, R. A. Journal of the Nigeria English Studies Associa-
      tion, No. 2 (November 1967), pp. 80-81.

THIS IS OUR CHANCE--Review

781   AXWORTHY, G. J. Ibadan, No. 1 (October 1957), pp. 27-28.

OLU IBUKUN

THE RETURN--Reviews

782   CADOGAN, LUCY. "New from Africa." New Statesman, 81,
      No. 2080 (29 January 1971), 155.

783   KAMIL, JILL. Lotus: Afro-Asian Writings, No. 12 (April
      1972), pp. 184-86.

Ike, Vincent Chukwuemeka

VINCENT CHUKWUEMEKA IKE

THE NAKED GODS--Reviews

784   MOORE, GERALD. Okike, 1, No. 3 (September 1972), 60-61.

785   Observer (31 May 1970), p. 30.

786   "Passage to Nigeria." Times Literary Supplement (18 June
       1970), p. 653.

THE POTTER'S WHEEL--Reviews

787   FAULKNER, PETER. Books and Bookmen, 19, No. 2 (November 1973),
       123.

788   Observer (23 September 1973), p. 36.

SUNSET AT DAWN--Reviews

789   JONES, D. A. N. "The Birth and Death of Biafra." Times Lit-
       erary Supplement (9 July 1976), p. 860.

790   MELLORS, JOHN. The Listener, 95, No. 2458 (20 May 1976), 654.

791   Observer (16 May 1976), p. 31.

TOADS FOR SUPPER--Reviews

792   ANIEBO, I. N. C. "The Straight and the Whorled." Nigeria
       Magazine, No. 86 (September 1965), pp. 218-21.

793   DATHORNE, O. R. Black Orpheus, No. 20 (August 1966),
       pp. 61-62.

794   EGBUNA, OBI B. "With No Pinch of Salt." New African, 4,
       No. 9 (November 1965), 213.

795   HAMILTON, ALEX. Books and Bookmen, 11, No. 3 (December 1965),
       53.

796   MORGAN, EDWIN. New Statesman, 69, No. 1783 (14 May 1965),
       772.

797   NAIPAUL, SHIVA. "Black and Ethereal." Books and Bookmen,
       16, No. 5 (February 1971), 41, 57.

Munonye, John

798   "Study-Hut Strains." Times Literary Supplement (8 April
       1965), p. 269.

799   W., K. West Africa, No. 2517 (28 August 1965), p. 967.

SEBASTIAN OKECHUKWU MEZU

BEHIND THE RISING SUN--Reviews

800   Choice, 10, No. 9 (November 1973), 1394.

801   JOWITT, DAVID. West Africa, No. 2838 (5 November 1971),
       p. 1297.

802   KERR, SUSAN. Books Abroad, 47, No. 2 (Spring 1973), 406-07.

803   "The Literature of Civil War." Times Literary Supplement
       (3 March 1972), p. 247.

804   SALAMAN, TAMARA. Observer (18 April 1971), p. 33.

THE TROPICAL DAWN--Review

805   GANT, LISBETH. Current Bibliography on African Affairs, 6,
       No. 1 (Winter 1973), 48.

JOHN MUNONYE

806   LINDFORS, BERNTH. "Interview with John Munonye." In his
       Dem-Say: Interviews with Eight Nigerian Writers. Austin:
       African and Afro-American Studies and Research Center,
       University of Texas, 1974, pp. 35-40.

A DANCER OF FORTUNE--Reviews

807   Choice, 13, No. 4 (June 1976), 527.

808   CLIFFORD, GAY. "Leaping Ahead." Times Literary Supplement
       (24 January 1975), p. 73.

809   Observer (16 February 1975), p. 30.

Munonye, John

<u>OBI</u>--Reviews

810   BARRON, LOUIS. <u>Library Journal</u>, 95, No. 11 (1 June 1970),
       2178-79.

811   <u>Choice</u>, 7, No. 11 (January 1971), 1516.

812   TRUTENAU, HELMUT M. J. "Custom Versus Christianity: Review
       of John Munonye: <u>Obi</u>." <u>The Legon Observer</u>, 5, No. 6
       (1970).

813   WANJALA, CHRIS L. "The Old and the New Do Not March."
       <u>Busara</u>, 3, No. 1 (1970), 56-59.

<u>OIL MAN OF OBANGE</u>--Reviews

814   <u>Choice</u>, 9, Nos. 5-6 (July-August 1972), 654.

815   N., M. <u>West Africa</u>, No. 2863 (28 April 1972), p. 518.

<u>THE ONLY SON</u>--Reviews

816   CARTER, DON. <u>African Literature Today</u>, No. 3 (1969),
       pp. 52-54.

817   D'CRUZ, VALERIE. <u>Nexus</u>, 1, No. 1 (1967), 43-45.

818   DIPOKO, MBELLA SONNE. <u>Présence Africaine</u>, No. 59 (1966),
       p. 162. <u>Présence Africaine</u>, English ed., 31 (1966), 155.

819   LARSON, CHARLES R. <u>Africa Report</u>, 12, No. 2 (February 1967),
       51-52.

820   OKAFOR, DUBEM. <u>The Muse</u>, No. 5 (May 1973), pp. 39-40.

821   <u>Times Literary Supplement</u> (21 July 1966), p. 629.

POL N. NDU

822   THOMAS, PETER. "The Unprogrammed Imagination (In Memoriam
       Pol Nana Ndu)." <u>Greenfield Review</u>, 5, Nos. 3-4 (Winter
       1976-1977), 5-6.

GOLGOTHA--Review

823   OKWU, EDWARD C.   <u>Ufahamu</u>, 4, No. 1 (Spring 1973), 162-68.

SONGS FOR SEERS (1960-1970)--Review

824   COLLINS, HAROLD.   <u>Books Abroad</u>, 50, No. 1 (Winter 1976),
       225-26.

NKEM NWANKWO

DANDA--Reviews

825   CASSIRER, THOMAS.   "Profile of a Jester."   <u>African Forum</u>, 1,
       No. 4 (Spring 1966), 128.

826   DATHORNE, O. R.   <u>Black Orpheus</u>, No. 18 (October 1965),
       pp. 59-60.

827   DORMAN, DAP.   <u>Drum</u> [Nigeria ed.], No. 163 (November 1964).

828   HUGH-JONES, STEPHEN.   <u>New Statesman</u>, 68, No. 1749
       (18 September 1964), 406.

829   "In Two Nigerian Villages."   <u>Times Literary Supplement</u>
       (17 September 1964), p. 853.

830   KILLAM, DOUGLAS.   "Recent African Fiction."   <u>Bulletin of the
       Association for African Literature in English</u>, No. 1
       (1964?), pp. 1-10.

831   OBIECHINA, EMMANUEL.   "Darkness and Light."   <u>Nigeria Magazine</u>,
       No. 84 (March 1965), pp. 61-63.

Danda--Review of Production

832   OLUSOLA, SEGUN.   "Danda Baptized."   <u>Nigeria Magazine</u>, No. 85
       (June 1965), pp. 153-56.
              Travelling Theatre production.

DANDA--Criticism

833   OBIECHINA, EMMANUEL.   "The Novel as Comedy: Nkem Nwankwo's
       <u>Danda</u>."   <u>The Muse</u>, No. 4 (May 1972), pp. 18-22.

Nwankwo, Nkem

834   TAIWO, OLADELE. "Danda Revisited: A Reassessment of
       Nwankwo's Jester." World Literature Written in English,
       13, No. 1 (April 1974), 7-16.

835   TAIWO, OLADELE. "Social Criticism." In his Culture and the
       Nigerian Novel. New York: St. Martin's Press, 1976,
       pp. 34-73.

MY MERCEDES IS BIGGER THAN YOURS--Reviews

836   Booklist, 72, No. 10 (15 January 1976), 667.

837   HALE, THOMAS A. Library Journal, 101, No. 3 (1 February
       1976), 547.

838   JONES, D. A. N. "This World and the Next." Times Literary
       Supplement (17 October 1975), p. 1238.

839   New Yorker, 51, No. 38 (10 November 1975), 190.

840   Observer (23 November 1975), p. 31.

GLORY OKOGBULE NWANODI

See Okogbule Wonodi p. 134.

FLORA NWAPA

841   EMENYONU, ERNEST N. "Who Does Flora Nwapa Write For?"
       African Literature Today, No. 7 (1975), pp. 28-33.
               Asserts that in an Igbo novel, what is said about the
       Igbo is as important as how it is said. Flora Nwapa suc-
       ceeds in both areas.

842   West Africa, No. 2874 (14 July 1972), p. 891.
               Nwapa's activities since the end of the war in Nigeria.

EFURU--Reviews

843   DARNBOROUGH, ANNE. "Quartet." The New African, 7, No. 1
       (March 1967), 10-11.

Nwapa, Flora

844   DIPOKO, MBELLA SONNE. Présence Africaine, No. 58 (1966),
         pp. 255-56. Présence Africaine, English ed., 30 (1966),
         249-50.

845   EMENYONU, ERNEST N. Ba Shiru (Spring 1970), pp. 58-61.

846   "How to Murder Your Husband." Times Literary Supplement
         (7 April 1966), p. 281.

847   IFEKA, CAROLINE. "The World of Women." Nigeria Magazine,
         No. 89 (June 1966), pp. 131-32, 141.

848   JONES, ELDRED. "Locale and Universe--Three Nigerian Novels."
         The Journal of Commonwealth Literature, No. 3 (July 1967),
         pp. 127-31.

849   PALMER, EUSTACE. African Literature Today, No. 1 (1968),
         pp. 56-58.

850   W., D. "Woman's World." West Africa, No. 2550 (16 April
         1966), p. 431.

EFURU--Criticism

851   CONDE, MARYSE. "Three Female Writers in Modern Africa: Flora
         Nwapa, Ama Ata Aidoo, and Grace Ogot." Présence Africaine,
         No. 82 (1972), pp. 132-43.

852   NANDAKUMAR, PREMA. "An Image of African Womanhood: A Study
         of Flora Nwapa's Efuru." Africa Quarterly, 11, No. 2
         (July-September 1971), 136-46.

853   SCHEUB, HAROLD. "Two African Women." Revue des Langues
         Vivantes, 37, Nos. 5-6 (1971), 545-58, 664-81.
         A study of Nwapa's Efuru and Amadi's The Concubine.

IDU--Review

854   JAMES, ADEOLA A. African Literature Today, No. 5 (1971),
         pp. 150-53.

THIS IS LAGOS AND OTHER STORIES-Review

855   OKORO, JERRY. "Tales of Lagos." West Africa, No. 2858
         (24 March 1972), pp. 353-54.

Nwoko, Demas

DEMAS NWOKO

856   HOSSMANN, IRMELINE. "Le Miracle du théâtre nigérien: Un
       Entretien avec Demas Nwoko." Afrique, No. 59
       (September 1966), pp. 36-40.

ONUORA NZEKWU

857   "Ibo Novelist." West Africa, No. 2331 (3 February 1962),
       p. 117.
          A portrait of Nzekwu and A Wand of Noble Wood.

858   KILLAM, G. D. "The Novels of Onuora Nzekwu." African Liter-
       ature Today, No. 5 (1971), pp. 21-40.
          Close analysis of three novels, each dealing with char-
       acters caught between two cultures.

859   LINDFORS, BERNTH. "The Africanization of Onuora Nzekwu."
       The Literary Half-Yearly, 13, No. 1 (January 1972), 93-103.
          Shows the progression of change in style from Nzekwu's
       first novel to Highlife for Lizards.

860   LINDFORS, BERNTH. "Oral Tradition and the Individual Literary
       Talent." Studies in the Novel, 4, No. 2 (Summer 1972),
       200-17. Reprinted in his Folklore in Nigerian Literature.
       New York: Africana, 1973, pp. 23-50.
          Combining of traditional and modern elements in the
       works of Tutuola, Nzekwu, and Achebe.

861   POVEY, JOHN. "The Novels of Onuora Nzekwu." Literature East
       and West, 12, No. 1 (March 1968), 68-84.

862   TAIWO, OLADELE. "Onuora Nzekwu and Elechi Amadi." In his
       Culture and the Nigerian Novel. New York: St. Martin's
       Press, 1976, pp. 181-209.

BLADE AMONG THE BOYS--Reviews

863   BRADBURY, MALCOLM. Punch, 243, No. 6361 (8 August 1962),
       211-12.

864   NWOGA, D. I. "Ibo Village Life." West Africa, No. 2356
       (28 July 1962), p. 827.

865   PRYSE, B. ELIZABETH. "Getting into Perspective." Nigeria
       Magazine, No. 74 (September 1962), pp. 83-85.

Nzekwu, Onuora

866   RICHARDSON, MAURICE. New Statesman, 64, No. 1637 (27 July
      1962), 121-22.

867   Times Literary Supplement (10 August 1962), p. 571.

868   Times Weekly Review (2 August 1962), p. 10.

869   WHITEMAN, KAYE. Présence Africaine, No. 50 (1964),
      pp. 269-70. Présence Africaine, English ed., 22 (1964),
      281-83.

BLADE AMONG THE BOYS--Criticism

870   JULY, ROBERT W. "African Literature and the African Person-
      ality." Black Orpheus, No. 14 (February 1964), pp. 33-45.
      Reprinted in Introduction to African Literature. Edited by
      Ulli Beier. Evanston, Ill.: Northwestern University
      Press, 1967, pp. 218-33. Reprinted in Modern Black Novel-
      ists: A Collection of Critical Essays. Edited by Michael
      G. Cooke. Englewood Cliffs, N.J.: Prentice-Hall, 1971,
      pp. 105-21.

HIGHLIFE FOR LIZARDS--Reviews

871   DORMAN, DAP. Drum [Nigeria ed.], (April 1966), [p. 32].

872   ECHERUO, MICHAEL J. C. "Attempting the Ritual Presentation."
      Nigeria Magazine, No. 87 (December 1965), pp. 288-91.

873   The Observer (14 November 1965), p. 28.

874   Times Literary Supplement (11 November 1965), p. 1007.

875   "Village Life." Insight, No. 13 (July-September 1966), p. 31.

WAND OF NOBLE WOOD--Reviews

876   ARAGBABALU, OMIDIJI. Black Orpheus, No. 11 (1962), pp. 66-67.

877   CAREW, JAN. Time and Tide, 42, No. 32 (10 August 1961), 1323.

878   MANNING, OLIVIA. Spectator, No. 6943 (21 July 1961), p. 99.

879   Times Literary Supplement (21 July 1961), p. 445.

880   Times Weekly Review (27 July 1961), p. 12.

881   WHITEMAN, KAYE. Présence Africaine, No. 50 (1964), pp. 269-70.
      Présence Africaine, English ed., 22 (1964), 281-83.

Nzekwu, Onuora

WAND OF NOBLE WOOD--Criticism

882   HORTON, ROBIN. "Three Nigerian Novelists." Nigeria Magazine,
      No. 70 (September 1961), pp. 218-24.

NWANONYE OBIECHINA

883   AGETUA, JOHN. "Interview with Nwanonye Obiechina." In his
      Interviews with Six Nigerian Writers. Benin City: Bendel
      Newspapers Corp., 1976?, pp. 24-29.

HUBERT OGUNDE

884   CLARK, EBUN. "Ogunde Theatre Content and Form." Black
      Orpheus, 3, Nos. 2-3 (October 1974-June 1975), 59-85.

885   CLARK, EBUN. "Ogunde Theatre: The Rise of Contemporary Pro-
      fessional Theatre in Nigeria, 1946-1972." Nigeria Magazine,
      No. 114 (December 1974), pp. 3-14; Nos. 115-116 (1975),
      pp. 9-24.

WALI OGUNYEMI

886   LAUTRE, MAXINE. "Wale Ogunyemi Interviewed by Maxine Lautre,
      Recorded May 1968 in Ibadan." Cultural Events in Africa,
      No. 51 (1969), pp. I-IV.

KIRIJI--Review of Production

887   ADELUGBA, DAPO. "Kiriji: The Concept of Theatre as Explora-
      tion." African Notes, 7, No. 1 (1971-1972), 107-16.
          Production by Department of Theatre Arts, University of
      Ibadan.

OBALUAYE: A MUSIC DRAMA--Review

888   LINDFORS, BERNTH. Books Abroad, 47, No. 4 (Autumn 1973), 816.

TANURE OJAIDE

CHILDREN OF IROKO--Criticism

889   OSUNDARE, OLUWANIYI. "Native, Serve Your River-God: The
       Poetry of Tanure Ojaide." Greenfield Review, 5, Nos. 3-4
       (1976-1977), 62-66.

GABRIEL OKARA

890   JABBI, BU-BUAKEI. West African Poems (Fifteen Analyses.)
       Freetown, Njala University College, 1974, pp. 40-48.
          Analyzes "One Night at Victoria Beach" and "Piano and
       Drums."

891   LINDFORS, BERNTH. "Interview with Gabriel Okara." World Lit-
       erature Written in English, 12, No. 2 (November 1973),
       132-41. Reprinted in his Dem-Say: Interviews with Eight
       Nigerian Writers. Austin: African and Afro-American
       Studies and Research Center, University of Texas, 1974,
       pp. 41-47.

892   McDOWELL, ROBERT E. "Three Nigerian Storytellers: Okara,
       Tutuola, and Ekwensi." Ball State University Forum, 10,
       No. 3 (Summer 1969), 67-75.
          The three authors' works have in common the influence
       of oral tradition and African characters without European
       contact.

893   NJOROGE, P. N. "Gabriel Okara: The Feeler of the Pulse of
       Africa's Soul." Busara, 5, No. 1 (1973), 48-56.
          The poetry of Okara expresses the soul of African
       society.

THE VOICE--Reviews

894   BANHAM, MARTIN. Books Abroad, 39, No. 3 (Summer 1965), 367.

895   BEIER, ULLI. Black Orpheus, No. 17 (June 1965), pp. 60-61.

896   CARTEY, WILFRED. African Forum, 1, No. 2 (Fall 1965), 110-12.

897   Choice, 8, No. 3 (May 1971), 398.

898   FARID, MAHER SHAFIK. Lotus: Afro-Asian Writings, No. 13
       (July 1972), pp. 180-83.

Okara, Gabriel

899   HUGH-JONES, STEPHEN. New Statesman, 68, No. 1749
      (18 September 1964), 406.

900   "In Two Nigerian Villages." Times Literary Supplement
      (17 September 1964), p. 853.

901   JOLLEY, M. Eastern Nigeria School Libraries Association
      Bulletin, 2, No. 1 (March 1966), 37.

902   KILLAM, DOUGLAS. "Recent African Fiction." Bulletin of the
      Association for African Literature in English, No. 1
      (1964?), pp. 1-10.

903   MACMILLAN, M. Journal of Commonwealth Literature, No. 1
      (September 1965), 174-75.

904   OBIECHINA, EMMANUEL. "Darkness and Light." Nigeria Magazine
      No. 84 (March 1965), pp. 61-63.

905   OTTAH, NELSON. "Mr. Okara's Tongue-Twister." Drum [Nigeria
      ed.], No. 166 (February 1965).

906   SITATI, PAUL G. "Okara's Amatu Revisited." Nexus, 2, No. 1
      (July 1968), 41-42.

907   WRIGHT, EDGAR. "Inside of Africa's Culture." East Africa
      Journal, 2, No. 2 (May 1965), 37-38.

THE VOICE--Criticism

908   ANOZIE, SUNDAY O. "The Problem of Communication in Two West
      African Novels." The Conch, 2, No. 1 (March 1970), 12-20.
         Compares Achebe and Okara in terms of themes, attitudes,
      toward English, and English usage.

909   ANOZIE, SUNDAY O. "The Theme of Alienation and Commitment in
      Okara's The Voice." Bulletin of the Association for Afri-
      can Literature in English, No. 3 (November 1965), pp. 54-67.

910   BURNESS, DONALD. "Stylistic Innovations and the Rhythm of
      African Life in Okara's The Voice." Journal of the New
      African Literature and the Arts, Nos. 13-14 (1972),
      pp. 13-20.

911   GOODLEY, NANCY C. "Two Levels of Meaning in Gabriel Okara's
      The Voice." CLA Journal, 19, No. 3 (March 1976), 312-17.
         Two interpretations of "it" in the novel.

912   LINDFORS, BERNTH. "Gabriel Okara: The Poet as Novelist."
      Pan-African Journal, 4, No. 4 (Fall 1971), 420-25.

913   OBIECHINA, E. N. "Art and Artifice in Okara's The Voice."
      Okike, 1, No. 3 (September 1972), 23-33.
             Technical devices which add to the novel's effectiveness.

914   PALMER, EUSTACE. "Gabriel Okara." In his An Introduction to
      the African Novel. New York: Africana, 1972, pp. 155-67.

915   ROSCOE, A. A. "Okara's Unheeded Voice--Explication and De-
      fence." Busara, 2, No. 1 (1969), 16-22. Reprinted in
      Standpoints on African Literature: Critical Essays. Ed-
      ited by Chris L. Wanjala. Nairobi: East African
      Literature Bureau, 1973, pp. 209-20.
             Experimental devices in The Voice.

916   SANDER, REINHARD. "A Political Interpretation of Gabriel
      Okara's The Voice." Omaba, No. 10 (March-April 1974),
      pp. 4-15.

917   SHIARELLA, J. "Gabriel Okara's The Voice: A Study in the
      Poetic Novel." Black Orpheus, 2, Nos. 5-6 (1970), 45-49.

918   TAIWO, OLADELE. "Social Criticism." In his Culture and the
      Nigerian Novel. New York: St. Martin's Press, 1976,
      pp. 34-73.

919   WALI, OBIAJUNWA. "The Individual and the Novel in Africa."
      Transition, 4, No. 18 (1965), 31-33.

CHRISTOPHER OKIGBO

920   ANOZIE, SUNDAY O. Christopher Okigbo: Creative Rhetoric.
      New York: Africana, 1972. 203 pp.

921   DATHORNE, O. R. "African Literature IV: Ritual and Ceremony
      in Okigbo's Poetry." Journal of Commonwealth Literature,
      No. 5 (July 1968), pp. 79-91.

922   "Death of Christopher Okigbo." Transition, 7, No. 33 (1967),
      18.
             A look at Okigbo's life and his views on literature.

923   DUERDEN, DENNIS. "Christopher Okigbo." In African Writers
      Talking. Edited by Cosmo Pieterse and Dennis Duerden. New
      York: Africana, 1972, pp. 139-43.
             Interview.

Okigbo, Christopher

924   EGUDU, ROMANUS. "Ezra Pound in African Poetry: Christopher
       Okigbo." Comparative Literature Studies, 8, No. 2 (June
       1971), 143-54.
          Ezra Pound's influence on Okigbo.

925   EGUDU, ROMANUS. "The Matter and Manner of Modern West African
       Poetry in English: A Study of Okigbo, Clark, Awoonor-
       Williams and Peters." Dissertation, Michigan State
       University, 1966.

926   ETHERTON, MICHAEL J. "Christopher Okigbo and African Tradi-
       tion." Zuka, No. 2 (May 1968), pp. 48-52.
          A response to Mazrui article. [930]

927   IZEVBAYE, DAN. "From Reality to the Dream: The Poetry of
       Christopher Okigbo." In The Critical Evaluation of African
       Poetry. Edited by Edgar Wright. Washington, D.C.:
       Inscape, 1973, pp. 120-48.

928   LESLIE, OMOLARA. "The Poetry of Christopher Okigbo: Its Evo-
       lution and Significance." Ufahamu, 4, No. 1 (Spring 1973),
       47-58. Reprinted in Studies in Black Literature, 4, No. 2
       (Summer 1973), 1-8. Reprinted in West Africa, No. 2912
       (2 April 1973), pp. 427, 429.

929   LUVAI, ARTHUR. "The Poetry of Wole Soyinka and Christopher
       Okigbo." In Standpoints on African Literature: Critical
       Essays. Edited by Chris L. Wanjala. Nairobi: East
       African Literature Bureau, 1973, pp. 284-301.

930   MAZRUI, ALI A. "Abstract Verse and African Tradition." Zuka,
       No. 1 (September 1967), pp. 47-49.
          Asserts that Okigbo's verse is too far removed from
       traditional modes of expression in Africa.

931   MOORE, GERALD. "Poetry and the Nigerian Crisis." Black
       Orpheus, 2, No. 3 (1968), 10-13.
          On Okigbo, Soyinka, and Clark.

932   MOORE, GERALD. "Vision and Fulfillment." In his The Chosen
       Tongue: English Writing in the Tropical World. New York:
       Harper & Row, 1970, pp. 163-76.

933   NKOSI, LEWIS. "Christopher Okigbo." In African Writers
       Talking. Edited by Cosmo Pieterse and Dennis Duerden.
       New York: Africana, 1972, pp. 133-38.
          Interview.

934   OKPAKU, JOSEPH O. O. "The Writer in Politics--Christopher
      Okigbo, Wole Soyinka, and the Nigerian Crisis." Journal
      of the New African Literature and the Arts, No. 4 (Fall
      1967), pp. 1-13.

935   POVEY, JOHN. "Epitaph to Christopher Okigbo." Africa Today,
      14, No. 6 (December 1967), 22-23.
         Themes and style of Okigbo's poetry.

936   SERUMAGA, ROBERT. "Christopher Okigbo Interviewed by Robert
      Serumaga on His Recent Visit to London." Cultural Events
      in Africa, No. 8 (July 1965), pp. I-IV. Reprinted in
      African Writers Talking. Edited by Cosmo Pieterse and
      Dennis Duerden. New York: Africana, 1972, pp. 143-47.

937   THEROUX, PAUL. "Christopher Okigbo." Transition, 5, No. 22
      (1965), 18-20.

938   THEROUX, PAUL. "Christopher Okigbo." In Introduction to
      Nigerian Literature. Edited by Bruce King. New York:
      Africana, 1972, pp. 135-51.

939   THOMAS, PETER. "A Personal Note on Christopher Okigbo."
      Compass, Nos. 5-6 (1974), pp. 25-26.

940   THOMAS, PETER. "'Ride Me Memories.' A Memorial Tribute to
      Christopher Okigbo (1932-1967)." African Arts/Arts
      d'Afrique, 1, No. 4 (Summer 1968), 68-70.
         Thomas reminisces about his friendship with Okigbo and
      mentions some of the influences on his poetry.

941   UDOEYOP, NYONG J. Three Nigerian Poets: A Critical Study of
      the Poetry of Soyinka, Clark and Okigbo. Ibadan: Ibadan
      University Press, 1973. 166 pp.

942   WHITELAW, MARJORY. "Interview with Christopher Okigbo, 1965.'
      The Journal of Commonwealth Literature, No. 9 (July 1970),
      pp. 28-37.

Distances--Criticism

943   ANOZIE, SUNDAY O. "A Structural Approach to Okigbo's 'Dis-
      tances.'" The Conch, 1, No. 1 (March 1969), 19-29. Re-
      printed in his Christopher Okigbo: Creative Rhetoric.
      New York: Africana, 1972, pp. 149-70.

944   EGUDU, R. N. "Okigbo's 'Distances': A Retreat from Christ
      to Idoto." The Conch, 5, Nos. 1-2 (1973), 29-42.

Okigbo, Christopher

Four Canzones--Criticism

945 ANOZIE, SUNDAY O. "Christopher Okigbo--A Creative Itinerary
     1957-1961." Présence Africaine, No. 64 (1967), pp. 158-66.
     Reprinted as "Creative Itinerary: Four Canzones: 1957-
     1961." In his Christopher Okigbo: Creative Rhetoric. New
     York: Africana, 1972, pp. 24-37.

946 DATHORNE, O. R. "Okigbo Understood--A Study of Two Poems."
     African Literature Today, No. 1 (1968), pp. 19-23.
         A detailed analysis of "Love Apart" ("Four Canzones")
     and "Overture" ("Heavensgate").

947 EGUDU, ROMANUS N. "Okigbo Misrepresented: Edwin Thumboo on
     'Love Apart.'" Présence Africaine, No. 76 (1970),
     pp. 187-93.
         Responds to Thumboo's criticism of Dathorne's interpre-
     tation of "Love Apart," a part of "Four Canzones." [949,
     946]

948 IKIDDEH, IME. African Literature Today, No. 2 (1969),
     pp. 55-56.
         A letter responding to Dathorne's analysis. [946]

949 THUMBOO, EDWIN. "Dathorne's Okigbo--A Dissenting View."
     African Literature Today, No. 3 (1969), pp. 44-49.
         A response to Dathorne's analysis. [946]

HEAVENSGATE--Reviews

950 CUTLER, BRUCE. Prairie Schooner, 38, No. 2 (Summer 1964),
     178-81.

951 JONES, LeROI. Poetry, 103, No. 6 (March 1964), 400.

952 KOLLVITZ, D. M. Quadrant, 7, No. 3 (Winter 1963), 83-84.

953 "Three Mbari Poets." Black Orpheus, No. 12 (1963?), pp. 46-50.

954 WILLIAMS, DENIS. "The Mbari Publications." Nigeria Magazine,
     No. 72 (December 1962), pp. 71-73.

HEAVENSGATE--Criticism

955 ANOZIE, SUNDAY O. "Okigbo's 'Heavensgate': A Study of Art as
     Ritual." Ibadan, No. 15 (March 1963), pp. 11-13. Re-
     printed as "Heavensgate." In his Christopher Okigbo:
     Creative Rhetoric. New York: Africana, 1972, pp. 41-62.

Okigbo, Christopher

956 DATHORNE, O. R. "Okigbo Understood--A Study of Two Poems."
African Literature Today, No. 1 (1968), pp. 19-23.
A detailed analysis of "Love Apart" ("Four Canzones")
and "Overture" ("Heavensgate").

957 EGUDU, ROMANUS. "Defence of Culture in the Poetry of
Christopher Okigbo." African Literature Today, No. 6
(1973), pp. 14-25.
Analysis of Heavensgate in terms of Okigbo's indigenous
religion and subsequent adoption of Christian religion.

958 IZEVBAYE, D. S. "Okigbo's Portrait of the Artist as a Sun-
bird: A Reading of Heavensgate (1962)." African Literature Today, No. 6 (1973), pp. 1-13.
Analyzes Heavensgate and compares to Labyrinths with
Paths of Thunder.

959 NDU, POL. "Mytho-Religious Roots of Modern Nigerian Poetry:
Christopher Okigbo--Heavensgate." Greenfield Review, 5,
Nos. 3-4 (Winter 1976-1977), 7-21.

960 THEROUX, PAUL. "Voices Out of the Skull--A Study of Six
African Poets." Black Orpheus, No. 20 (August 1966),
pp. 41-58. Reprinted in Introduction to African Literature. Edited by Ulli Beier. Evanston, Ill.: Northwestern
University Press, 1967, pp. 110-31.

961 THUMBOO, EDWIN. "Dathorne's Okigbo--A Dissenting View."
African Literature Today, No. 3 (1969), pp. 44-49.
A response to Dathorne's analysis. [946]

LABYRINTHS WITH PATHS OF THUNDER--Reviews

962 CALDER, ANGUS. New Statesman, 83, No. 2145 (28 April 1972),
564.

963 MORSBERGER, ROBERT E. Books Abroad, 46, No. 2 (Spring 1972),
347-48.

964 PHILCOX, RICHARD. Présence Africaine, No. 80 (1971),
pp. 169-70.

965 THOMAS, PETER. "Shadows of Prophecy." Journal of Modern
African Studies, 11, No. 2 (June 1973), 339-45.

966 VINCENT, T. Black Orpheus, 2, No. 7 (1971-1972), 31-33.

967 W., K. "The Okigbo Legend." West Africa, No. 2871
(23 June 1972), 793.

Okigbo, Christopher

LABYRINTHS WITH PATHS OF THUNDER--Criticism

968   STANTON, ROBERT J.   "Poet as Martyr: West Africa's Christopher
       Okigbo, and His Labyrinths with Paths of Thunder." Studies
       in Black Literature, 7, No. 1 (Winter 1976), 10-14.

LIMITS--Reviews

969   DATHORNE, O. R.   Black Orpheus, No. 15 (August 1964),
       pp. 59-60.

970   RUKEYSER, M. "Two African Poets." African Forum, 1, No. 1
       (Summer 1965), 145-48.

LIMITS--Criticism

971   ADEDEJI, JOEL A. "A Dramatic Approach to Okigbo's Limits."
       The Conch, 3, No. 1 (March 1971), 45-58.
           Demonstrates how improvisation can help to elucidate
       Okigbo's poetry.

972   NWOGA, DONATUS I. "Okigbo's Limits: An Approach to Meaning."
       Journal of Commonwealth Literature, 7, No. 1 (June 1972),
       92-101.

973   THEROUX, PAUL. "Voices Out of the Skull: A Study of Six
       African Poets." Black Orpheus, No. 20 (August 1966),
       pp. 41-58. Reprinted in Introduction to African Litera-
       ture. Edited by Ulli Beier. Evanston, Ill.: Northwestern
       University Press, 1967, pp. 110-31.

Silences--Criticism

974   ANOZIE, SUNDAY O. "Poetry and Empirical Logic: A Corre-
       spondence Theory of Truth in Okigbo's Laments." The
       Conch, 2, No. 1 (March 1970), 54-65.
           Shows that Okigbo's poetry has its own logistics. The
       structure of "The Lament of the Drums" is used as an
       example.

JOSEPH OKPAKU

Born Astride the Grave--Criticism

975   NWOZOMUDO, BENEDICTA. "An Epoch: A Critique of 'Born
       Astride the Grave.'" Journal of the New African Litera-
       ture, No. 1 (Spring 1966), pp. 12-13.

ISIDORE OKPEWHO

THE LAST DUTY--Reviews

976   SAGE, LORNA. "White Captive." Observer (12 September 1976),
       p. 28.

977   WOOD, ADOLF. "The Woes of War." Times Literary Supplement
       (1 October 1976), p. 1229.

THE VICTIMS--Reviews

978   BENDOW, BURTON. The Nation, 214, No. 12 (20 March 1972),
       376-77.

979   CAREW, JAN. New York Times Book Review (2 April 1972),
       pp. 7, 14-15.

980   N., P. "A Classical Tragedy." West Africa, No. 2796
       (9-15 January 1971), p. 41.

D. O. OLAGOKE

THE INCORRUPTIBLE JUDGE--Review

981   MGBEMENE, A. E. D. Eastern Nigeria School Libraries Associa-
       tion Bulletin, 2, No. 1 (March 1966), 37, 39.

THE IROKO-MAN AND THE WOODCARVER--Review

982   MGBEMENE, A. E. D. Eastern Nigeria School Libraries Associa-
       tion Bulletin, 2, No. 1 (March 1966), 37, 39.

KOLE OMOTOSO

983   AGETUA, JOHN. "Interview with Kole Omotoso." In his Inter-
       views with Six Nigerian Writers. Benin City: Bendel
       Newspapers Corp., 1976?, pp. 10-16.

984   BOZIMO, WILLY. "Dr. Omotoso: Novelist and Academician."
       Spear (July 1976), pp. 34, 38.

985   BOZIMO, WILLY. "The Literary World of Kole Omotoso." Spear
       (September 1976), pp. 35-36.

Omotoso, Kole

986   DOHAN, OYADO. "Kole Omotoso in Review." Indigo, 2, No. 3
       (March 1975), 14, 16, 18-19.

987   "Kole Omotoso." African Book Publishing Record, 2, No. 1
       (January 1976), 12-14.
          Interview.

988   LINDFORS, BERNTH. "Kole Omotoso Interviewed by Bernth
       Lindfors in Ibadan, May 14, 1973." Cultural Events in
       Africa, No. 103 (1975), pp. 2-12. Reprinted in his
       Dem-Say: Interviews with Eight Nigerian Writers. Austin:
       African and Afro-American Studies and Research Center, Uni-
       versity of Texas, 1974, pp. 48-56.

989   WALDER, DENNIS. "Interview with Kole Omotoso." Transition,
       9, No. 44 (1974), 45-57.

THE COMBAT--Reviews

990   CONATEH, SWAEBOU. Ndaanan, 4, Nos. 1-2 (March/September 1974),
       64-65.

991   IHEAKARAM, PAUL O. Afriscope, 4, No. 4 (April 1974), 49.

THE EDIFICE--Reviews

992   Afriscope, 4, No. 3 (March 1974), 47, 49.

993   Choice, 9, No. 11 (January 1973), 1453.

994   CONATEH, SWAEBOU. Ndaanan, 4, Nos. 1-2 (March-September 1974),
       64-65.

995   W., D. "Passing Through." West Africa, No. 2912
       (2 April 1973), p. 436.

SACRIFICE--Review

996   AKOBI, KOFI. Afriscope, 5, No. 8 (August 1975), 53, 55.

DENNIS CHUKUDE OSADEBAY

997   KONWEA, FRED OKONICHA. Personality Profile: Chief Dennis
       Osadebay, Administrator of Mid-Western Nigeria. Lagos:
       Nigerian National Press, 1964?. 11 pp.

Rotimi, Ola

AFRICA SINGS--Criticism

998   ANOZIE, SUNDAY O. "Two Nigerian Poets." African Writer, 1,
       No. 1 (August 1962), 3-4, 26-28.

FEMI OSOFISAN

KOLERA KOLEJ--Review of Production

999   OMOTOSO, KOLE. "Kolera Kolej on Stage." Afriscope, 5, No. 6
       (June 1975), 49.
              University of Ibadan.

OLA ROTIMI

1000   ASEIN, SAMUEL OMO. "Ola Rotimi and the New Dramatic Movement
       at Ife." Bulletin of Black Theatre, 1, No. 2 (Winter 1972),
       4-5.

1001   FOLARIN, M. "Ola Rotimi Interviewed." New Theatre Magazine,
       12, No. 2 (1972), 5-7.

1002   LINDFORS, BERNTH. "Interview with Ola Rotimi." In his Dem-
       Say: Interviews with Eight Nigerian Writers. Austin:
       African and Afro-American Studies and Research Center,
       University of Texas, 1974, pp. 57-68.

1003   WREN, ROBERT M. "Ola Rotimi: A Major New Talent." Africa
       Report, 18, No. 5 (September-October 1973), 29-31.

THE GODS ARE NOT TO BLAME--Reviews

1004   BISHOP, TERRY. "African Oedipus." West Africa, No. 2850
       (28 January 1972), p. 97.

1005   RENDLE, ADRIAN. Drama, No. 103 (Winter 1971), p. 77.

THE GODS ARE NOT TO BLAME--Reviews of Production

1006   ADELUGBA, DAPO. Ibadan, No. 27 (October 1969), pp. 49-50.
              Ile-Ife, December 1968.

Rotimi, Ola

1007   BADEJO, PETER. "Premier Production: The Gods Are Not to
        Blame." African Arts/Arts d'Afrique, 3, No. 2 (Winter
        1970), 64-65.
            Ile-Ife, December 1968.

KURUNMI--Review

1008   RENDLE, ADRIAN. Drama, No. 108 (Spring 1973), pp. 82-84.

KURUNMI--Review of Production

1009   OKE, OLA. "Tragedy Beautifully Rendered." Nigeria Magazine,
        No. 102 (September-November 1969), pp. 525-27.

OVONRAMWEN NOGBAISI--Review of Production

1010   ASEIN, SAMUEL O. "The Tragic Grandeur of Ovonramwen Nogbaisi."
        Nigeria Magazine, Nos. 110-112 (1974), pp. 40-49.
            Fourth Ife Festival of the Arts, 1971.

The Prodigal--Review of Production

1011   AJOLORE, O. "Last Evening at Ori Olokun." Nigeria Magazine,
        No. 102 (September-November 1969), pp. 528-29.
            Second Ife Festival of the Arts.

ZULU SOFOLA

1012   AGETUA, JOHN. "Interview with Zulu Sofola." In his Inter-
        views with Six Nigerian Writers. Benin City: Bendel
        Newspapers Corp., 1976?, pp. 18-23.

1013   OMOTOSO, KOLE. "Interview with Playwright Zulu Sofola."
        Afriscope, 3, No. 12 (1973), 59-60.

WOLE SOYINKA

1014   AGETUA, JOHN. "Interview with Wole Soyinka." In his Inter-
        views with Six Nigerian Writers. Benin City: Bendel
        Newspapers Corp., 1976?, pp. 38-57.

Soyinka, Wole

1015   ALLEN, SAMUEL W. "Two African Writers: Soyinka and
       Senghor." African Studies Association meeting paper,
       1966. Negro Digest, 16, No. 8 (June 1967), 54–67.
         Contrasts themes and philosophy toward negritude in the
       works of Soyinka and Senghor.

1016   AMADI, LAWRENCE EKPEMA. "Historical and Cultural Elements in
       the Works of Chinua Achebe and Wole Soyinka: Instructional
       Resources for the Teacher of Nigerian Literature and Cul-
       ture." Dissertation, University of Missouri, 1972.

1017   ASALACHE, KHADAMBI. "The Making of a Poet: Wole Soyinka."
       Présence Africaine, No. 67 (1968), pp. 172–74.

1018   BANHAM, MARTIN. "Playwright/Producer/Actor/Academic: Wole
       Soyinka in the Nigerian Theatre." New Theatre Magazine,
       12, No. 2 (1972), 10–11.
         Soyinka's topics, craftsmanship, and audience.

1019   BARTHOLD, BONNIE JO. "Three West African Novelists: Chinua
       Achebe, Wole Soyinka, and Ayi Kwei Armah." Dissertation,
       University of Arizona, 1975.

1020   BODUNRIN, A. "Wole Soyinka: Poet, Satirist and Political
       Neophyte." African Statesman, 2, No. 3 (November 1967),
       19, 21, 23–27.

1021   COLLINGS, REX. "Wole Soyinka; A Personal View." New States-
       man, 76, No. 1971 (20 December 1968), 879. Reprinted as
       "A Propos." African Arts/Arts d'Afrique, 2, No. 3
       (Spring 1969), 82–84.

1022   DAMERON, CHARLES F., JR. "An Assault on Tyranny: Soyinka's
       Recent Writings." Africa Today, 23, No. 2 (April–June
       1976), 65–67.
         Traces the subject of tyranny and its alternatives in
       Soyinka's works.

1023   DAVIS, ANN B. "Dramatic Theory of Wole Soyinka." Ba Shiru,
       7, No. 1 (1976), 1–11.

1024   DUERDEN, DENNIS. "African Sharpshooter." New Society, 8,
       No. 219 (8 December 1966), 879.
         Soyinka's career and the criticism of African culture
       in his plays.

Soyinka, Wole

1025   DUERDEN, DENNIS. "A Triumph for Wole Soyinka." New Society
       (28 April 1966), pp. 21-22.
           Soyinka and his Kongi's Harvest at the First World Fes-
       tival of Negro Arts in Dakar.

1026   DUERDEN, DENNIS. "Wole Soyinka." In African Writers Talking.
       Edited by Cosmo Pieterse and Dennis Duerden. New York:
       Africana, 1972, pp. 178-80.
       Interview.

1027   DUODU, CAMERON. "Did He . . . Or Didn't He?" The Guardian
       (24 July 1968), p. 6.
           Praises Soyinka's talents and decries his imprisonment.

1028   DUODU, CAMERON. "Wole Soyinka: His Talent and the Mystery of
       His Fate." Legon Observer, 3, No. 16 (2-15 August 1968),
       17-18.

1029   EGUDU, R. N. "The Idyll Sham: Ezra Pound and Nigerian Wole
       Soyinka on War." Paideuma, 5, No. 1 (Spring 1976), 31-41.
           Compares Pound poem "Hugh Selwyn Mauberley" (Sections IV
       and V) with Soyinka's "Flowers for My Land" and "For
       Christopher Okigbo."

1030   EKO, EBELE OFOMO. "The Critical Reception of Amos Tutuola,
       Chinua Achebe and Wole Soyinka in England and America
       1952-1974." Dissertation, University of North Carolina
       at Greensboro, 1974.

1031   ENEKWE, OSSIE ONUORA. "Wole Soyinka as a Novelist." Okike,
       No. 9 (December 1975), pp. 72-86.
           Compares Soyinka's diction and obscurity with James
       Joyce's.

1032   ESSLIN, MARTIN. "A Major Poetic Dramatist--Wole Soyinka."
       New Theatre Magazine, 12, No. 2 (1972), 9-10.
           Short survey of Soyinka's plays.

1033   EZEOKOLI, VICTORIA CHINWENMA. "African Theatre--A Nigerian
       Prototype." Dissertation, Yale University, 1972.
           Form and language in the dramatic works of Clark and
       Soyinka.

1034   FEARN, MARIANNE. "Modern Drama of Africa--Form and Content:
       A Study of Four Playwrights." Dissertation, Northwestern
       University, 1974.

1035 FERGUSON, JOHN. "Nigerian Drama in English." Modern Drama,
     11, No. 1 (May 1968), 10-28.
     Includes discussion of the works of Clark and Soyinka.

1036 GATES, LOUIS S. "An Interview with Soyinka." Black World,
     24, No. 10 (August 1975), 30-48.

1037 GIBBS, JAMES M. "Bio-Bibliography: Wole Soyinka." Africana
     Library Journal, 3, No. 1 (Spring 1972), 15-22.

1038 GIBBS, JAMES. "Date-Line on Soyinka." New Theatre Magazine,
     12, No. 2 (1972), 12-14.
     Chronology of Soyinka's life.

1039 GIBBS, JAMES. "Interpreting the Interpreter." Joliso, 1,
     No. 2 (1973), 110-26.
     Examines Soyinka's critical writings and relates them to
     this work as a creative artist.

1040 GIBBS, JAMES. "Soyinka and Ghana." Legon Observer, 6, No. 15
     (16-29 July 1971), 22, 24.
     Soyinka's relations with Nkrumah and anti-Nkrumaism in
     his plays.

1041 GIBBS, JAMES. "Wole Soyinka and Radio." Legon Observer, 8,
     No. 21 (19 October-1 November 1973), 508, 510.
     Soyinka's work for radio, especially Camwood on the
     Leaves and The Detainee.

1042 GRAHAM-WHITE, ANTHONY. "The Plays of J. P. Clark and Wole
     Soyinka." In his The Drama of Black Africa. New York:
     Samuel French, 1974, pp. 117-45.

1043 GURR, ANDREW J. "Third World Drama: Soyinka and Tragedy."
     Joliso, 2, No. 2 (1974), 13-20. Reprinted in Journal of
     Commonwealth Literature, 10, No. 3 (April 1976), 45-52.

1044 GUSSOW, MEL. "Play from a Jail Cell Tested at Drama Parley."
     New York Times (20 July 1970), p. 22.
     Soyinka's participation in Playwrights Conference
     (O'Neill Center, Waterford, Connecticut) with Madmen and
     Specialists.

1045 HADDAD, MARJORIE ARLENE. "Pollution and Purification in the
     Novels and Plays of Wole Soyinka, Chinua Achebe, and John
     Pepper Clark." Dissertation, New York University, 1976.

Soyinka, Wole

1046   HEYWOOD, ANNEMARIE. "The Fox's Dance: The Staging of
        Soyinka's Plays." African Literature Today, No. 8 (1976),
        pp. 42-51.

1047   "History and African Conscience." Africa: International
        Business, Economic and Political Monthly, No. 58 (June
        1976), pp. 109-10.
            Interview.

1048   IDAPO, COZ. "The Ways of a Rebel." Drum [Nigeria ed.],
        No. 147 (July 1963), pp. 36-37.
            Describes Soyinka's Ibadan residence.

1049   "Interview with Prof. Wole Soyinka." Afriscope, 6, No. 7
        (July 1976), 39-40.

1050   IRELE, ABIOLA. "An Evening with Soyinka." Legon Observer, 4,
        No. 5 (28 February 1969), 20, 22.
            Reviews extracts from Soyinka's works presented in
        Legon.

1051   IRELE, ABIOLA. "The Season of a Mind: Wole Soyinka and the
        Nigerian Crisis." The Benin Review, No. 1 (June 1974),
        pp. 111-22.
            Soyinka's social awareness as reflected in his works.

1052   IRELE, A. "Tradition and the Yoruba Writer: D. O. Fagunwa,
        Amos Tutuola and Wole Soyinka." Odu, No. 11 (January
        1975), pp. 75-100.

1053   IZEVBAYE, DAN S. "Soyinka's Black Orpheus." African Studies
        Association meeting paper, 1974. In Neo-African Literature
        and Culture: Essays in Memory of Janheinz Jahn. Edited by
        Bernth Lindfors and Ulla Schild. Weisbaden: Heymann,
        1976, pp. 147-58.

1054   JABBI, BU-BUAKEI. West African Poems (Fifteen Analyses).
        Freetown: Njala University College, 1974, pp. 22-32.
            Analyzes "Abiku," "Death in the Dawn," and "Season."

1055   JEYIFOUS, BIODUN. "Wole Soyinka." Transition, 8, No. 42
        (1973), 62-64.
            Interview.

1056   JONES, ELDRED D. "The Essential Soyinka." In Introduction
        to Nigerian Literature. Edited by Bruce King. New York:
        Africana, 1972, pp. 113-34.

Soyinka, Wole

1057   JONES, ELDRED. "Progress and Civilization in the Work of Wole
        Soyinka." In Perspectives on African Literature. Edited
        by Christopher Heywood. New York: Africana, 1971,
        pp. 129-37.

1058   JONES, ELDRED D. Wole Soyinka. New York: Twayne, 1973.
        183 pp.

1059   JONES, ELDRED D. "Wole Soyinka: Critical Approaches." In
        The Critical Evaluation of African Literature. Edited by
        Edgar Wright. Washington, D.C.: Inscape, 1976, pp. 51-72.
        Soyinka's plays.

1060   KATAMBA, FRANCIS. "Death and Man in the Earlier Works of Wole
        Soyinka." Journal of Commonwealth Literature, 9, No. 3
        (April 1975), 63-71.

1061   KHAZNADAR, CHERIF. "Efficacité de Wole Soyinka." Jeune
        Afrique, No. 585 (25 March 1972), p. 48.
        Themes of Soyinka's plays.

1062   KING, BRUCE. "Two Nigerian Writers: Tutuola and Soyinka."
        The Southern Review, 6, No. 3 (July 1970), 843-48.

1063   LABURTHE-TOLRA, PHILIPPE. "Soyinka, ou la tigritude." Abbia,
        No. 19 (March 1968), pp. 55-67.

1064   LANE, BRIGITTE D. "Theatre for the Unborn: Analysis of the
        Plays of Wole Soyinka, 1957-1974." Thesis, University of
        Kansas, 1974.

1065   LA PIN, DEIRDRE A. "The Festival Plays of Wole Soyinka."
        Thesis, University of Wisconsin, 1971.

1066   LAPPING, BRIAN. "The Road to Somewhere." The Guardian
        (13 September 1965), p. 7.
        Soyinka's background.

1067   LARSON, CHARLES R. "Wole Soyinka: Nigeria's Leading Social
        Critic." New York Times Book Review (24 December 1972),
        pp. 6-7, 10.
        Social criticism in Soyinka's works, especially in Mad-
        men and Specialists.

1068   LAURENCE, MARGARET. "Voices of Life, Dance of Death." In her
        Long Drums and Cannons: Nigerian Dramatists and Novelists.
        New York: Praeger, 1969, pp. 11-76.
        Interpretative analysis of his works.

Soyinka, Wole

1069   LINDFORS, BERNTH. "The Early Writings of Wole Soyinka."
        Journal of African Studies, 2, No. 1 (Spring 1975), 64-86.
        Reprinted in his Critical Perspectives on Nigerian Litera-
        tures. Washington, D.C.: Three Continents Press, 1976,
        pp. 169-94.
            Traces Soyinka's writing career from 1954 to 1963, be-
        fore his first books were published.

1070   LINDFORS, BERNTH. "Wole Soyinka and the Horses of Speech."
        In Essays on African Literature. Spectrum Monograph Series
        in the Arts and Sciences, 3. Edited by W. L. Ballard.
        Atlanta: School of Arts and Sciences, Georgia State Uni-
        versity, 1973, pp. 79-87. Reprinted in his Folklore in
        Nigerian Literature. New York: Africana, 1973, pp. 105-15.
            Proverbs in Soyinka's plays.

1071   LINDFORS, BERNTH. "Wole Soyinka Talking through His Hat."
        African Studies Association meeting paper, 1974. In Com-
        monwealth Literature and the Modern World. Edited by Hena
        Maes-Jelinek. Brussels: Didier, 1975, pp. 115-25.
            Soyinka's work in Nigerian radio and television in the
        early 1960's.

1072   LINDFORS, BERNTH. "Wole Soyinka, When Are You Coming Home?"
        Yale French Studies, No. 53 (1976), pp. 197-210.
            Critical of Soyinka for writing plays that can be appre-
        ciated only by a small elite group.

1073   LUVAI, ARTHUR. "The Poetry of Wole Soyinka and Christopher
        Okigbo." In Standpoints on African Literature: Critical
        Essays. Edited by Chris L. Wanjala. Nairobi: East
        African Literature Bureau, 1973, pp. 284-301.

1074   MACEBUH, STANLEY. "Poetics and the Mythic Imagination."
        Transition, No. 50 (October 1975-March 1976), pp. 79-84.
            Defends Soyinka's poetry against Chinweizu's and
        Madubuike's criticisms. [28]

1075   MACLEAN, UNA. "Soyinka's International Drama." Black
        Orpheus, No. 15 (August 1964), pp. 46-51.
            Soyinka's drama, although containing Nigerian refer-
        ences, has a universal appeal without the use of exotic
        effects.

1076   MAXIMIN, DANIEL. "Le Théâtre de Wole Soyinka." Présence
        Africaine, No. 79 (1971), pp. 103-17.

Soyinka, Wole

1077 McCARTNEY, BARNEY CHARLES. "The Traditional Satiric Method
      and Matter of Wole Soyinka and Chinua Achebe." Disserta-
      tion, University of Texas at Austin, 1976.

1078 McNEIVE, KAY. "Wole Soyinka, Nigerian Dramatist." Thesis,
      University of Kansas, 1967.

1079 MOORE, GERALD. "The Meaning of Sacrifice." In his The Chosen
      Tongue: English Writing in the Tropical World. New York:
      Harper & Row, 1970, pp. 177-90.
          Sacrificial death in The Road and The Interpreters.

1080 MOORE, GERALD. "Poetry and the Nigerian Crisis." Black
      Orpheus, 2, No. 3 (1968), 10-13.
          On Okigbo, Soyinka, and Clark.

1081 MOORE, GERALD. Wole Soyinka. New York: Africana, 1971.
      114 pp.

1082 MOOTRY, MARIA K. "Soyinka and Yoruba Mythology." Ba Shiru,
      7, No. 1 (1976), 23-32.

1083 MORELL, KAREN L. In Person: Achebe, Awoonor, and Soyinka at
      the University of Washington. Seattle: Institute for
      Comparative and Foreign Area Studies, University of
      Washington, 1975. 163 pp.
          Lecture by Soyinka on "Drama and the Revolutionary
      Ideal" and discussion.

1084 MPHAHLELE, EZEKIEL. "Wole Soyinka." In African Writers
      Talking. Edited by Cosmo Pieterse and Dennis Duerden.
      New York: Africana, 1972, pp. 169-71.
          Interview.

1085 "National Dramatist." West Africa, No. 2481 (19 December
      1964), p. 1417.
          Biographical portrait.

1086 NAZARETH, PETER. "The Politics of Wole Soyinka." In his
      Literature and Society in Modern Africa: Essays on Liter-
      ature. Nairobi: East African Literature Bureau, 1972,
      pp. 58-75.

1087 NDIAYE, J.-P. "Bachir Touré et Wole Soyinka: Deux voies (et
      deux voix) pour une dramaturgie africaine." Jeune Afrique,
      No. 544 (8 June 1971), pp. 51-56.
          Interview.

Soyinka, Wole

1088   NGUGI, JAMES. "Satire in Nigeria: Chinua Achebe, T. M. Aluko
       and Wole Soyinka." In Protest and Conflict in African Lit-
       erature. Edited by Cosmo Pieterse and Donald Munro. New
       York: Africana, 1969, pp. 56-69. Reprinted in his [Ngugi
       wa Thiong'o] Homecoming: Essays on African and Caribbean
       Literature. New York: Lawrence Hill, 1973, pp. 55-66.
           Satire which serves to criticize social and political
       conditions in Nigeria.

1089   NKOSI, LEWIS. "Wole Soyinka." In African Writers Talking.
       Edited by Cosmo Pieterse and Dennis Duerden. New York:
       Africana, 1972, pp. 171-77.
           Interview.

1090   NWOGA, D. I. "Poetry as Revelation: Wole Soyinka." The
       Conch, 6, Nos. 1-2 (1974), 60-79.
           Analyzes style and content in Soyinka's poetry.

1091   OGUNBA, OYIN. "Language in an Age of Transition: Shakespeare
       and Soyinka." Journal of the Nigeria English Studies Asso-
       ciation, 6, No. 1 (May 1974), 107-18.
           Both Soyinka and Shakespeare are successful at showing a
       diversity of human types through language.

1092   OGUNBA, OYIN. The Movement of Transition: A Study of the
       Plays of Wole Soyinka. Ibadan: Ibadan University Press,
       1975. 235 pp.

1093   OGUNBA, OYIN. "Traditional Content of the Plays of Wole
       Soyinka." African Literature Today, No. 4 (1970),
       pp. 2-18; No. 5 (1971), pp. 106-15.
           Describes the use of Yoruba expressions and songs, the
       festivals, and traditional sanctions in Soyinka's plays.

1094   OGUNGBESAN, KOLAWOLE. "Wole Soyinka: The Past and the Vi-
       sionary Writer." In A Celebration of Black and African
       Writing. Edited by Bruce A. King and Kolawole Ogungbesan.
       New York: Oxford University Press, 1975, pp. 175-88.

1095   OLAFIOYE, TAYO. "Cultural Conventions in Soyinka's Art."
       Ba Shiru, 7, No. 1 (1976), 67-70.
           Yoruba cultural conventions in Soyinka's satirical
       plays.

1096   OSOFISAN, FEMI. "Soyinka in Paris." West Africa, No. 2875
       (21 July 1972), p. 935.
           Describes an evening at the Theatre des Nations in
       Paris where Soyinka presented an extract from A Dance in
       the Forest.

100

Soyinka, Wole

1097   POVEY, JOHN. "Wole Soyinka and the Nigerian Drama." Tri-
        quarterly, No. 5 (1966), pp. 129-35.

1098   PRIEBE, RICHARD KARL. "The Development of a Mythic Conscious-
        ness in West African Literature." Dissertation, University
        of Texas at Austin, 1973.

1099   PURISCH, CHRISTINE WINTER. "Wole Soyinka: A Critical Analy-
        sis of His Poetry." Thesis, Duquesne University, 1972.

1100   RECKORD, BARRY. "Notes on Two Nigerian Playwrights." The New
        African, 4, No. 7 (September 1965), 171.

1101   RICARD, ALAIN. "Les Limites de l'étude d'influence: théâtre
        nigérian et théâtre anglais." Proceedings of the 6th Con-
        gress of the International Comparative Literature Associa-
        tion. Stuttgart: Kunst and Wissen, Erich Bieber, 1975,
        pp. 635-38.

1102   RICARD, ALAIN. Théâtre et nationalisme: Wole Soyinka et
        LeRoi Jones. Paris: Présence Africaine, 1972. 235 pp.

1103   RICARD, ALAIN. "Wole Soyinka and LeRoi Jones: An Attempt at
        a Comparative Study of Their Concept of Nationalism in
        Drama." African Studies Association annual meeting paper,
        1969. [Not published, but available for purchase from
        African Studies Association.]

1104   SOYINKA, WOLE. "Gbohun-Gbohun: The Nigerian Playwright Wole
        Soyinka on His Dealings with the BBC." The Listener, 88,
        No. 2275 (2 November 1972), 581-83.

1105   STAUDT, KATHLEEN. "The Characterization of Women by Soyinka
        and Armah." Afras Review, 1, No. 1 (Summer 1975), 40-43.
        Women in Soyinka's novels.

1106   TAIWO, O. "Two Incantations to 'Abiku.'" Nigeria Magazine,
        No. 106 (September-November 1970), pp. 219-24.
        Compares poems entitled "Abiku" by Clark and Soyinka.
        Describes this Nigerian concept.

1107   TUCKER, MARTIN. "West African Literature: The Second De-
        cade." Africa Today, 13, No. 5 (May 1966), 7-9; 13, No. 6
        (June 1966), 7-8.
        Survey of Soyinka's plays.

1108   UDOEYOP, NYONG J. Three Nigerian Poets: A Critical Study of
        the Poetry of Soyinka, Clark and Okigbo. Ibadan: Ibadan
        University Press, 1973. 166 pp.

Soyinka, Wole

1109   WEALES, GERALD. "Wole Soyinka: Yoruba Plays for All Tribes."
       The Hollins Critic, 11, No. 5 (December 1974), 1-13.

1110   WHITE, WALTER F. "Oluwole Soyinka Alive?" L'Afrique
       Actuelle, Nos. 34-35 (February 1969), pp. 51-52.
           Tells of announcement of Soyinka's death in British
       newspapers.

1111   WHITE, WALTER F. "Wole Soyinka Detained Again." L'Afrique
       Actuelle, No. 22 (November 1967), p. 43.
           Quotes articles written by Soyinka and describes the
       actions which caused Soyinka to be detained.

1112   "Why Did Wole Quit?" Afriscope, 2, No. 5 (May 1972), 13, 15.
           Why Soyinka resigned his position as head of the Theatre
       Arts Department at the University of Ibadan.

1113   WILKINSON, NICK. "Audience, Dream World and Wole Soyinka's
       Plays (Exploring an Idea)." The Muse, No. 6 (May 1974),
       38-44.

1114   "Wole Soyinka: il faut appeler la guerre par son nom."
       Bingo, No. 206 (March 1970), p. 37.
           Soyinka's political activities and his imprisonment.

1115   "Wole Soyinka: What Is He to Us?" Afriscope, 4, No. 5
       (May 1974), 58-60.
           Soyinka's thoughts on language and politics and his in-
       fluence on young writers.

1116   "Young Dramatist is Earning the Title of Nigeria's Bernard
       Shaw." Drum [Nigeria ed.] March 1961, p. 27.

THE BACCHAE OF EURIPIDES--Reviews

1117   Booklist, 71, No. 9 (1 January 1975), 439.

1118   Choice, 11, No. 12 (February 1975), 1772.

1119   KNOX, BERNARD. "Greek for the Greekless." New York Review of
       Books, 23, No. 1 (5 February 1976), 11-12.

1120   LUDDY, THOMAS E. Library Journal, 100, No. 1 (1 January 1975),
       62.

1121   "Myth-Mesh." Times Literary Supplement (1 March 1974), p. 214.

Criticism of Nigerian Authors

Soyinka, Wole

THE BACCHAE OF EURIPIDES--Review of Production

1122   LAHR, JOHN. Plays and Players, 21, No. 1 (October 1973), 59.
        National Theatre, London.

THE BACCHAE OF EURIPIDES--Criticism

1123   GIBBS, JAMES. "Brook in Nigeria: Soyinka in London." Odi,
        1, No. 3 (October 1973), 16-19.

BEFORE THE BLACKOUT--Reviews

1124   MAHOOD, M. M. New Theatre Magazine, 12, No. 2 (1972), 26.

1125   W., K. "Soyinka Before and After." West Africa, No. 2868
        (2 June 1972), p. 692.

BEFORE THE BLACKOUT--Review of Production

1126   Cultural Events in Africa, No. 7 (June 1965), pp. 5-6.

CAMWOOD ON THE LEAVES--Reviews

1127   "The Battle of the Beach." Times Literary Supplement
        (8 February 1974), p. 138.

1128   RENDLE, ADRIAN. Drama, No. 112 (Spring 1974), pp. 81-83.

COLLECTED PLAYS, 1--Reviews

1129   Booklist, 70, No. 15 (1 April 1974), 850.

1130   Choice, 11, Nos. 5-6 (July-August 1974), 768.

1131   RENDLE, ADRIAN. Drama, No. 111 (Winter 1973), pp. 87-88.

COLLECTED PLAYS, 2--Reviews

1132   Afriscope, 5, No. 8 (August 1975), 55.

1133   COLEBY, JOHN. Drama, No. 116 (Spring 1975), pp. 91-93.

A DANCE OF THE FORESTS--Reviews

1134   BANHAM, MARTIN. Books Abroad, 38, No. 1 (Winter 1964), 92.

1135   BEIER, ULLI. Black Orpheus, No. 8 (1960), pp. 57-58.

Soyinka, Wole

1136   BLAIR, D. S. English Studies in Africa, 7, No. 1 (March
        1964), 128-31.

1137   HOLMES, TIMOTHY. "Five Soyinka Plays." The New African, 2,
        No. 6 (13 July 1963), 112-13.

A DANCE OF THE FORESTS--Reviews of Productions

1138   BARE. African Horizon, No. 2 (January 1961), pp. 8-11.
        Performances in Lagos and Ibadan.

1139   COCKSHOTT, UNA. Ibadan, No. 10 (November 1960), pp. 30-32.
        At University College, Ibadan.

A DANCE OF THE FORESTS--Criticism

1140   GASTON, JESSIE. "A Dance of the Forests: A Critique."
        Busara, 7, No. 1 (1975), 33-40.

1141   GIBBS, JAMES. "The Origins of A Dance of the Forests."
        African Literature Today, No. 8 (1976), pp. 66-71.

1142   GLEASON, JUDITH. "Out of the Irony of Words." Transition, 4,
        No. 18 (1965), 34-38.

1143   WATSON, IAN. "Soyinka's Dance of the Forests." Transition,
        6, No. 27 (1966), 24-26.

1144   WILKINSON, NICK. "Demoke's Choice in Soyinka's A Dance of
        the Forests." Journal of Commonwealth Literature, 10,
        No. 3 (April 1976), 22-27.

DEATH AND THE KING'S HORSEMAN--Reviews

1145   BANHAM, MARTIN. "New Soyinka Play." Journal of Commonwealth
        Literature, 10, No. 3 (April 1976), 80-81.

1146   Booklist, 72, No. 20 (15 June 1976), 1443-44.

1147   Choice, 13, No. 7 (September 1976), 837.

1148   COLEBY, JOHN. Drama, No. 119 (Winter 1975), p. 87.

1149   HALE, THOMAS A. Library Journal, 101, No. 10 (15 May 1976),
        1222.

1150   JONES, D. A. N. "This World and the Next." Times Literary
        Supplement (17 October 1975), p. 1238.

Soyinka, Wole

FIVE PLAYS--Reviews

1151   Choice, 2, No. 12 (February 1966), 870.

1152   HILL, GEOFFREY. "Nigerian Plays." Journal of Commonwealth
         Literature, No. 1 (September 1965), pp. 172-74.

1153   JONES, D. A. N. New Statesman, 69, No. 1768 (29 January
         1965), 164.

1154   "Third World Stage." Times Literary Supplement (1 April
         1965), p. 252.

1155   WRIGHT, EDGAR. East Africa Journal, 2, No. 7 (November 1965),
         35-36, 38.

1156   YANKOWITZ, SUSAN. "The Plays of Wole Soyinka." African
         Forum, 1, No. 4 (Spring 1966), 129-33.

FIVE PLAYS--Criticism

1157   ELATE, MIKE E. "The Intellectual as an Artist in Soyinka's
         Five Plays." In Mélanges africains. Yaounde: Editions
         Pedagogiques Afrique-Contact, 1973, pp. 299-327.

1158   ESSLIN, MARTIN. "Two African Playwrights." Black Orpheus,
         No. 19 (March 1966), pp. 33-39. Reprinted as "Two Nigerian
         Playwrights." In Introduction to African Literature. Ed-
         ited by Ulli Beier. Evanston, Ill.: Northwestern Univer-
         sity Press, 1967, pp. 255-62.
            Includes discussion of Clark's and Soyinka's use of the
         English language.

IDANRE AND OTHER POEMS--Reviews

1159   AIDOO, AMA ATA. "Poets and Ostriches." West Africa,
         No. 2641 (13 January 1968), pp. 40-41.

1160   AYAGERE, SOLOMON. Nigeria Magazine, No. 96 (March 1968),
         p. 52.

1161   CARRUTH, HAYDEN. Hudson Review, 23, No. 1 (Spring 1970),
         191-92.

1162   Choice, 6, No. 7 (September 1969), 826.

1163   CUSHMAN, JEROME. Library Journal, 94, No. 3 (1 February 1969),
         555.

Soyinka, Wole

1164   HOLMES, RICHARD. "Poets, Men, Gods, and Heroes." The Times
        (18 November 1967), p. 22.

1165   ISICHEI, ELIZABETH. African Affairs, 68, No. 271 (April
        1969), 176.

1166   IYENGAR, K. R. SRINIVASA. Africa Quarterly, 9, No. 2
        (July–September 1969), 182–84.

1167   JONES, D. A. N. New York Review of Books, 13, No. 2
        (31 July 1969), 8, 10.

1168   PRESS, JOHN. Punch, 254, No. 6648 (7 February 1968), 211.

1169   Publishers Weekly, 194, No. 8 (19 August 1968), 73.

1170   ROSS, ALAN. London Magazine, 7, No. 11 (February 1968),
        99–100.

1171   SMITH, JOHN. "Areas of Discontent." Poetry Review, 61, No. 1
        (Spring 1970), 89–90.

1172   THORPE, MICHAEL. English Studies, 49, No. 3 (June 1968), 280.

1173   Times Literary Supplement (18 January 1968), p. 62.

1174   TUCKER, MARTIN. "African Genesis." The Nation, 209, No. 16
        (10 November 1969), 510–12.

IDANRE AND OTHER POEMS--Criticism

1175   FATOBA, FEMI. "Idanre: An Appreciation." Nigeria Magazine,
        Nos. 107–109 (December 1970–August 1971), pp. 101–12.
        Analysis of the poem.

1176   JONES, ELDRED D. "Naked into Harvest-Tide: The Harvest
        Image in Soyinka's Idanre." African Literature Today,
        No. 6 (1973), pp. 145–51.

1177   ROSCOE, ADRIAN A. "Soyinka as Poet." In his Mother is Gold:
        A Study in West African Literature. Cambridge: University
        Press, 1971, pp. 48–63. Reprinted in Readings in Common-
        wealth Literature. Edited by William Walsh. Oxford:
        Clarendon Press, 1973, pp. 163–80.

Soyinka, Wole

1178   SALT, M. J. "Mr. Wilson's Interpretation of a Soyinka Poem."
       Journal of Commonwealth Literature, 9, No. 3 (April 1975),
       76-78.
            Disagrees with Wilson's interpretation of the poem
       "Dawn." [1180]

1179   SCOTT, CHRISTOPHER. "Some Aspects of the Structural Unity of
       'Idanre.'" World Literature Written in English, No. 20
       (November 1971), pp. 11-14.

1180   WILSON, RODERICK. "Complexity and Confusion in Soyinka's
       Shorter Poems." Journal of Commonwealth Literature, 8,
       No. 1 (June 1973), 69-80.

THE INTERPRETERS--Reviews

1181   ANIEBO, I. N. C. "The Straight and the Whorled." Nigeria
       Magazine, No. 86 (September 1965), pp. 218-21.

1182   CAVISTON, JOHN F. Library Journal, 97, No. 17 (1 October
       1972), 3183.

1183   "Chameleon Clues." Insight, No. 13 (July-September 1966),
       pp. 31-32.

1184   "Chameleon Clues." Times Literary Supplement (1 April 1965),
       p. 260.

1185   CHEUSE, ALAN. "Prophet of Death and 'Voidancy.'" The Nation,
       215, No. 9 (2 October 1972), 284-85.

1186   Choice, 9, No. 11 (January 1973), 1454.

1187   HEMMINGS, F. W. J. New Statesman, 69, No. 1782 (7 May 1965),
       733-34.

1188   KING, BRUCE. Black Orpheus, No. 19 (March 1966), p. 55.

1189   LASK, THOMAS. New York Times (11 August 1972), p. 26.

1190   MALKIN, MARY ANN O'BRIAN. Antiquarian Bookman, 37
       (7 February 1966), 526.

1191   MOHAMEDALI, HAMIDA. "Reconciled Extremes." Nexus, 1, No. 3
       (January 1968), 37-39.

1192   MOORE, GERALD. "The First Novel." The New African, 4, No. 7
       (September 1965), 156.

Soyinka, Wole

1193   NWOGA, DONATUS. Ibadan, No. 22 (June 1966), pp. 62-63.

1194   OTTAH, NELSON. "Wole Soyinka's Brilliant Interpretation."
       Drum [Nigeria ed.], No. 170 (June 1965).

1195   THOMPSON, JOHN. "Dublin, Paris, Ibadan, Iowa City." African
       Forum, 1, No. 2 (Fall 1965), 108-09.

1196   WARDLE, I. Observer (21 March 1965), p. 26.

THE INTERPRETERS--Criticism

1197   ACKLEY, DONALD G. "Wole Soyinka's The Interpreters." Black
       Orpheus, 2, Nos. 5-6 (1970), 50-57.

1198   JONES, ELDRED. "The Interpreters, Wole Soyinka: Reading
       Notes." African Literature Today, No. 2 (1969), pp. 42-50.
           Discusses narrative technique, characters, and language
       in The Interpreters. Includes reading notes with page
       references.

1199   JONES, ELDRED. "Interpreting The Interpreters." Bulletin of
       the Association for African Literature in English, No. 4
       (March 1966), pp. 13-18.

1200   JONES, ELDRED D. "A Note on Editing The Interpreters, a Novel
       by Wole Soyinka." In Editing Twentieth Century Texts. Ed-
       ited by Francess G. Halpenny. Toronto: University of
       Toronto Press, 1972, pp. 93-101.

1201   KIIRU, MUCHUGU. "Elitism in Soyinka's The Interpreters."
       Busara, 6, No. 1 (1974), 12-16.
           The Interpreters fails to portray the feelings of ordi-
       nary people struggling to survive.

1202   LARSON, CHARLES R. "The Novel of the Future: Wole Soyinka
       and Ayi Kwei Armah." In his The Emergence of African Fic-
       tion. Bloomington: Indiana University Press, 1971,
       pp. 242-77.

1203   NIEMI, RICHARD. "Will the Beautyful Ones Ever Be Born?" The
       Pan-Africanist, No. 3 (December 1971), pp. 18-23.
           Examines the imagery of waste.

1204   OBIECHINA, EMMANUEL. "Post-Independence Disillusionment in
       Three African Novels." In Neo-African Literature and Cul-
       ture: Essays in Memory of Janheinz Jahn. Edited by Bernth
       Lindfors and Ulla Schild. Wiesbaden: Heymann, 1976,
       pp. 119-46.

Soyinka, Wole

1205   RUTIMIRWA, ALEX. "Exaltation of Art: Interpreting Soyinka's
       The Interpreters (An Introduction)." Dhana, 5, No. 1
       (1975), 24-28.
            Refutes criticism that The Interpreters lacks structural
       and thematic unity.

1206   SCANLON, MARIT. "Symbolism in The Interpreters." The Mirror
       (1972-1973?), pp. 29-34.

1207   STEWART, JAMES. "Return to His Native Village." Busara, 2,
       No. 1 (1968), 37-39.

The Invention--Reviews of Production

1208   "African Playwright and Poet." The Times (2 November 1959),
       p. 3.
            London, Royal Court Theatre.

1209   BRIEN, ALAN. "Where Spades are Trumps." The Spectator, 203,
       No. 6854 (6 November 1959), 629-30.
            London, Royal Court Theatre.

The Invention--Criticism

1210   LARSON, CHARLES R. "Soyinka's First Play: 'The Invention.'"
       Africa Today, 18, No. 4 (October 1971), 80-83.

THE JERO PLAYS--Reviews

1211   "The Battle of the Beach." Times Literary Supplement
       (8 February 1974), p. 138.

1212   No entry

1213   GIBBS, J. Books Abroad, 48, No. 4 (Autumn 1974), 834-35.

1214   MELLORS, JOHN. London Magazine, 14, No. 1 (April-May 1974),
       135-36.

KONGI'S HARVEST--Reviews

1215   ARDEN, JOHN. New Theatre Magazine, 12, No. 2 (1972), 25-26.

1216   BANHAM, MARTIN. "Nigerian Dramatists." Journal of Common-
       wealth Literature, No. 7 (July 1969), pp. 132-36.

1217   DIPOKO, MBELLA SONNE. Présence Africaine, No. 63 (1967),
       pp. 262-63.

Soyinka, Wole

1218   THORPE, MICHAEL. English Studies, 49, No. 3 (June 1968),
       275.

1219   W., K. West Africa, No. 2609 (3 June 1967), pp. 723, 725.

KONGI'S HARVEST--Reviews of Productions

1220   BERRY, BOYD M. Ibadan, No. 23 (October 1966), pp. 53-55.
       University of Ibadan production.

1221   CLURMAN, HAROLD. The Nation, 206, No. 18 (29 April 1968),
       581.
       New York, Negro Ensemble Company production.

1222   DATHORNE, O. R. Black Orpheus, No. 21 (April 1967), pp. 60-61.
       Lagos, Federal Palace Hotel, August 1965.

1223   KERR, WALTER. "Tantalizing but Blurred." New York Times
       (21 April 1968), II, p. 5.
       New York, Negro Ensemble Company production.

1224   KROLL, JACK. "Caesar in Africa." Newsweek, 71, No. 18
       (29 April 1968), 93.
       New York, Negro Ensemble Company production.

1225   LEWIS, THEOPHILUS. America, 118, No. 19 (11 May 1968),
       651-52.
       New York, Negro Ensemble Company production.

1226   OKE, OLA. "Tragedy Beautifully Rendered." Nigeria Magazine,
       No. 102 (September-November 1969), pp. 525-27.
       At Second Ife Festival of the Arts.

1227   OLIVER, EDITH. The New Yorker, 44, No. 10 (27 April 1968),
       86, 91.
       New York, Negro Ensemble Company production.

1228   SULLIVAN, DAN. "Confrontation in a Tribe." New York Times
       (15 April 1968), p. 49.
       New York, Negro Ensemble Company production.

1229   Time, 91 (26 April 1968), 97.
       New York, Negro Ensemble Company production.

KONGI'S HARVEST--Criticism

1230   ATILADE, DAVID. "Kongi's Harvest, and the Men Who Made the
       Film." Interlink, 6, No. 4 (October-December 1970), 4-5,
       7-12, 14-15.

Soyinka, Wole

The filming of Kongi's Harvest and interviews with Ossie Davis, director, and Francis Oladele, producer.

1231 BROWN, NIGEL. Notes on Wole Soyinka's Kongi's Harvest. Nairobi: Heinemann Educational Books, 1973. 48 pp.

1232 GIBBS, JAMES. Study Aid to Kongi's Harvest. London: Rex Collings, 1973. 46 pp.

1233 LARSON, CHARLES R. "Nigerian Drama Comes of Age." Africa Report, 13, No. 5 (May 1968), 55-57.
      Discusses Clark's Ozidi and Soyinka's Kongi's Harvest as evidence of a new age of Nigerian drama.

1234 MBUGHUNI, P. "A Grain of Wheat, Song of Lawino, Song of Ocol, and Kongi's Harvest." Umma, 5, No. 1 (1975), 64-74.
      Political values as a theme.

1235 MSHENGU. "Kongi's Harvest by Wole Soyinka." S'ketsh' (Summer 1973), pp. 33-34.

1236 SEVERAC, ALAIN. "Technique dramatique et message politique dans Kongi's Harvest." Université de Dakar Annales de la Faculté des Lettres et Sciences Humaines, No. 4 (1974), pp. 77-111.

THE LION AND THE JEWEL--Reviews

1237 BANHAM, MARTIN. Books Abroad, 38, No. 1 (Winter 1964), 92.

1238 BLAIR, D. S. English Studies in Africa, 7, No. 1 (March 1964), 128-31.

1239 GREEN, ROBERT. "The Clashing Old and New." The Nation, 201, No. 11 (11 October 1965), 224-25.

1240 HOLMES, TIMOTHY. "Five Soyinka Plays." The New African, 2, No. 6 (13 July 1963), 112-13.

1241 KUNENE, MAZISI and COSMO PIETERSE. "Soyinka in London: Two Writers in London Assess The Lion and the Jewel." The New African, 6, No. 1 (March 1967), 9-10.

1242 NAZARETH, PETER. Transition, 4, No. 10 (September 1963), 47-48.

Soyinka, Wole

THE LION AND THE JEWEL--Reviews of Productions

1243   AKANJI, SANGODARE. "Criticism of The Lion and the Jewel and
            The Swamp Dwellers." Black Orpheus, No. 6 (November 1959),
            pp. 50-51.
                University of Ibadan production.

1244   BANJO, AYO. "The Lion and the Jewel at the Arts Theatre."
            Ibadan, No. 26 (February 1969), pp. 82-83.
                University of Ibadan production.

1245   BRYDEN, RONALD. "African Sophistication." The Observer
            (18 December 1966), p. 20.
                London, Royal Court Theatre.

1246   DARLINGTON, W. A. "Simple Parable of African Life." The
            Daily Telegraph (13 December 1966), p. 15.
                London, Royal Court Theatre.

1247   HOBSON, HAROLD. "The Lion and the Jewel from Africa."
            Christian Science Monitor (6 January 1967), p. 4.
                London, Royal Court Theatre.

1248   HOPE-WALLACE, PHILIP. The Guardian (13 December 1966), p. 7.
                London, Royal Court Theatre.

1249   JONES, D. A. N. New Statesman, 72, No. 1866 (16 December
            1966), 916.
                London, Royal Court Theatre.

1250   NGUGI, JAMES. Transition, 3, No. 12 (January-February 1964),
            55.
                Makerere College Dramatic Society production.

1251   "Nigerian Play for Court Theatre." The Times (28 November
            1966), p. 6.
                Announcement of opening and personnel involved.

1252   "Sheer Ingenuity of Soyinka's Plot." The Times (13 December
            1966), p. 6.
                London, Royal Court Theatre.

1253   S'ketsh' (Summer 1974-1975), pp. 36-37.
                Production in South Africa by the Alice Seminary
            Dramsoc.

1254   TAYLOR, JOHN RUSSELL. "Avoiding the Insulting." Plays and
            Players, 14, No. 5 (February 1967), 14-15.
                London, Royal Court Theatre.

Criticism of Nigerian Authors

Soyinka, Wole

THE LION AND THE JEWEL--Criticism

1255 DAILLY, CHRISTOPHE. "Conflit de civilisations dans Le Lion et
la perle de Wole Soyinka." Annales de l'Université
d'Abidjan, 7D (1974), 169-78. Reprinted in Recherche,
Pédagogie et Culture, 4, No. 21 (1976), 41-44.

1256 ERAPU, LABAN. Notes on Wole Soyinka's "The Lion and the
Jewel." Nairobi: Heinemann Educational Books, 1976.
44 pp.

1257 KRONENFELD, J. Z. "The 'Communalistic' African and the 'In-
dividualistic' Westerner: Some Comments on Misleading Gen-
eralizations in Western Criticism of Soyinka and Achebe."
Research in African Literatures, 6, No. 2 (Fall 1975),
199-225. Reprinted in Critical Perspectives on Nigerian
Literature. Edited by Bernth Lindfors. Washington, D.C.:
Three Continents Press, 1976, pp. 243-70.

1258 McELROY, HILDA. "Some Stylistic Expressions, Attitudes and
Patterns in Contemporary African Drama." The Pan Afri-
canist, No. 3 (December 1971), pp. 39-41.

1259 MOHMED, A. "The Lion and the Jewel Reconsidered: Observa-
tions on the Relation between Character and Language in the
Play." The Mirror (1972-1973?), pp. 34-41.

1260 POVEY, JOHN F. "Wole Soyinka: Two Nigerian Comedies." Comparative Drama, 3, No. 2 (Summer 1969), 120-32.

1261 RICARD, ALAIN. "Les Paradoxes de Wole Soyinka." Présence
Africaine, No. 72 (1969), pp. 202-11.

1262 RICHARD, RENE. "La Peinture sociale dans Le Lion et la perle
de Wole Soyinka." In Actes du Colloque sur le théâtre
negro-africain. Paris: Présence Africaine, 1971,
pp. 105-12.

1263 RICHARD, RENE. "Les Problèmes sociaux à travers les person-
nages de la pièce de Wole Soyinka: Le Lion et la perle
(Nigeria)." In Tradition et innovation: littérature et
paralittérature. Paris: Didier, 1975, pp. 341-49.

1264 RICHARD, R. "Théâtre nigérian anglophone." Etudes
Anglaises, 25 (January-March 1972), 199-206.

113

Soyinka, Wole

1265 TAIWO, OLADELE. "Wole Soyinka: The Lion and the Jewel."
     In his An Introduction to West African Literature. London:
     Nelson, 1967, pp. 163-76.

1266 TAUBMAN, HOWARD. "A Nigerian Looks at 'Progress.'" New York
     Times (18 April 1965), II, p. 1.

1267 WALKER, BILL. "Mime in The Lion and the Jewel." World Liter-
     ature Written in English, 12, No. 1 (April 1973), 37-44.

MADMEN AND SPECIALISTS--Reviews

1268 AB Bookman's Weekly, 49 (19 June 1972), 2331.

1269 "Anti-War Play." Literary Half-Yearly, 14, No. 1 (January
     1973), 166-68.

1270 BANHAM, MARTIN. "Darkness and Threat." Journal of Common-
     wealth Literature, 8, No. 1 (June 1973), 124-26.

1271 CALDER, ANGUS. New Statesman, 83, No. 2145 (28 April 1972),
     564.

1272 Choice, 9, No. 11 (January 1973), 1454.

1273 "The Devotees of As." Times Literary Supplement (31 December
     1971), p. 1632.

1274 MENKITI, IFEANYI. Library Journal, 97, No. 15 (1 September
     1972), 2748.

1275 RENDLE, ADRIAN. Drama, No. 104 (Spring 1972), p. 81.

1276 W., K. "Soyinka Before and After." West Africa, No. 2868
     (2 June 1972), pp. 692-93.

MADMEN AND SPECIALISTS--Reviews of Production

1277 BUNCE, ALAN. "Soyinka's Nigerian Play: Madmen and Special-
     ists." Christian Science Monitor (15 August 1970), p. 12.
         Theatre Arts Company of the University of Ibadan pro-
     duction at O'Neill Center, Waterford, Conn.

1278 GUSSOW, MEL. "Psychological Play from Nigeria." New York
     Times (3 August 1970), p. 38. Reprinted in Cultural Events
     in Africa, No. 65 (August 1970), pp. 2-3.
         Theatre Arts Company of the University of Ibadan pro-
     duction at O'Neill Center, Waterford, Conn.

Soyinka, Wole

MADMEN AND SPECIALISTS--Criticism

1279   BAMIKUNLE, ADEREMI. "What Is 'As'? Why 'As'? A Thematic
        Exegesis of Wole Soyinka's Madmen and Specialists." Work
        in Progress, 2 (1973), 126-49.

1280   BERRY, BOYD M. "On Looking at Madmen and Specialists." Pan
        African Journal, 5, No. 4 (Winter 1972), 461-71.

1281   GUSSOW, M. "The Making of a Play." Topic, No. 58 (1971?),
        pp. 29-31.
            Soyinka's production at the O'Neill Center in
        Connecticut.

1282   IYENGAR, K. R. SRINIVASA. "Soyinka's Latest Play." Literary
        Half-Yearly, 17, No. 2 (July 1976), 3-17.

1283   JOHNSON, CHRIS. "Performance and Role-Playing in Soyinka's
        Madmen and Specialists." Journal of Commonwealth Litera-
        ture, 10, No. 3 (April 1976), 27-33.

1284   McCARTNEY, BARNEY C. "Traditional Satire in Wole Soyinka's
        Madmen and Specialists." African Studies Association an-
        nual meeting paper, 1974. World Literature Written in
        English, 14, No. 2 (November 1975), 506-13.

POEMS FROM PRISON--Review

1285   JONES, ELDRED D. African Literature Today, No. 4 (1970),
        pp. 58-59.

THE ROAD--Reviews

1286   Choice, 3, Nos. 5-6 (July-August 1966), 423.

1287   DUNCAN, BERNICE G. Books Abroad, 40, No. 3 (Summer 1966),
        360-61.

1288   "Keep Off the Road." Times Literary Supplement (10 June
        1965), p. 476.

1289   PIETERSE, COSMO. "Dramatic Riches." Journal of Commonwealth
        Literature, No. 2 (December 1966), pp. 168-71.

1290   SHELTON, AUSTIN JESSE, JR. Africa Report, 11, No. 5 (May
        1966), 66.

1291   YANKOWITZ, SUSAN. "The Plays of Wole Soyinka." African
        Forum, 1, No. 4 (Spring 1966), 129-33.

Criticism of Nigerian Authors

Soyinka, Wole

THE ROAD--Reviews of Production

(All of the reviews below are of the production at Theatre Royal, London, for the Commonwealth Arts Festival.)

1292   BILLINGTON, MICHAEL. "First Night." Plays and Players, 13, No. 2 (November 1965), 34.

1293   BRYDEN, RONALD. "The Asphalt God." New Statesman, 70, No. 1802 (24 September 1965), 460-61.

1294   FAY, GERALD. The Guardian (15 September 1965), p. 7.

1295   GILLIATT, PENELOPE. "A Nigerian Original." The Observer (19 September 1965), p. 25.

1296   HOBSON, HAROLD. "Nigerian Drama in Premiere." Christian Science Monitor (22 September 1965), p. 4.

1297   M., J. A. "Clark & Soyinka at the Commonwealth Arts Festival." The New African, 4, No. 8 (October 1965), 195.

1298   PIETERSE, COSMO. Cultural Events in Africa, No. 10 (September 1965), pp. 4-5.

1299   "Rumbustious Start to Festival." The Times (15 September 1965), p. 14.

1300   SERUMAGA, ROBERT. "The Road, by Wole Soyinka: Reaction of the Critics." Cultural Events in Africa, No. 11 (October 1965), Supplement pp. I-II.

1301   SHORTER, ERIC. "Nigerian Author of Talent." The Daily Telegraph (15 September 1965), p. 18.

1302   "Soyinka's Hard Road." The Observer (19 September 1965), p. 23.

1303   SPURLING, HILARY. The Spectator (24 September 1965), p. 380.

1304   West Africa, No. 2520 (18 September 1965), p. 1061.

1305   West Africa, No. 2523 (9 October 1965), p. 1133.

THE ROAD--Criticism

1306   AMANKULOR, JAMES NDUKA. "Dramatic Technique and Meaning in The Road." Ba Shiru, 7, No. 1 (1976), 53-58.

Soyinka, Wole

1307   IZEVBAYE, D. S.   "Language and Meaning in Soyinka's The
       Road." African Literature Today, No. 8 (1976), pp. 52-65.

1308   MOYO, S. PHANISO. "The Road, a Slice of the Yoruba Pantheon."
       Ba Shiru (Fall 1970-Spring 1971), pp. 89-93.
       Sacrifice as the central theme.

SEASON OF ANOMY--Reviews

1309   ACKROYD, PETER. Spectator, 231, No. 7590 (15 December 1973),
       787.

1310   CIMA, RICHARD. Library Journal, 99, No. 12 (15 June 1974),
       1732.

1311   DAVIES, RUSSELL. "Swallowing the Lexicon." Observer
       (9 December 1973), p. 36.

1312   "Dragon Slayer." Times Literary Supplement (14 December 1973),
       p. 1529.

1313   MELLORS, JOHN. London Magazine, 14, No. 1 (April-May 1974),
       135-36.

1314   OMOTOSO, KOLE. "Mere Mirrors of Annihilation." Afriscope,
       4, No. 7 (July 1974), 42-43.

1315   SCHMIDT, NANCY J. The Conch Review of Books, 3, No. 1
       (March 1975), 269-71.

1316   SEGAL, AARON. Africa Today, 22, No. 4 (October-December 1975),
       92.

1317   SHRAPNEL, NORMAN. "Plots before the Eyes." Guardian Weekly,
       110 (5 January 1974), 25.

1318   TARROW-MORDI, DITA. Africa: International Business, Economic
       and Political Monthly, No. 32 (April 1974), pp. 62-63.

1319   WRIGHT, EDGAR. African Literature Today, No. 8 (1976),
       pp. 115-20.

A SHUTTLE IN THE CRYPT--Reviews

1320   CALDER, ANGUS. New Statesman, 84, No. 2177 (8 December 1972),
       866.

1321   Choice, 9, No. 11 (January 1973), 1454.

Soyinka, Wole

1322   CLUYSENAAR, ANNE. Stand, 14, No. 1 (n.d.), pp. 71-72.

1323   ESHLEMAN, CLAYTON. Library Journal, 97, No. 15 (1 September
        1972), 2737.

1324   GAKWANDI, ARTHUR. "The Little Victories and the Greater
        Loss." Dhana, 2, No. 2 (1972), 61-63.

1325   GANT, LISBETH. A Current Bibliography on African Affairs, 6,
        No. 2 (Spring 1973), 206.

1326   JONES, ELDRED. African Literature Today, No. 6 (1973),
        pp. 174-75.

1327   MALKIN, MARY ANN O'BRIAN. AB Bookman's Yearbook, Part 1,
        (1972), p. 25.

1328   O'HARA, T. Best Sellers, 32 (15 October 1972), 327.

1329   PRIEBE, RICHARD. Books Abroad, 47, No. 2 (Spring 1973), 407.

A SHUTTLE IN THE CRYPT--Criticism

1330   TIGHE, C. "In Detentio Preventione in Aeternum: Soyinka's
        A Shuttle in the Crypt." The Journal of Commonwealth Lit-
        erature, 10, No. 3 (April 1976), 9-22.

The Strong Breed--Reviews of Productions

1331   CLURMAN, HAROLD. The Nation, 205, No. 19 (4 December 1967),
        606.
        New York, Greenwich Mews Theatre.

1332   "Infectious Humanity." Time (17 November 1967), pp. 50, 52.
        New York, Greenwich Mews Theatre.

1333   OLIVER, EDITH. The New Yorker, 43, No. 39 (18 November 1967),
        133-34.
        New York, Greenwich Mews Theatre.

1334   WARDLE, IRVING. "Clash of Values." The Times (27 November
        1968), p. 8a.
        London, Harmony Culture Theatre Group production at
        Mercury Theatre.

1335   WEALES, GERALD. The Reporter, 38, No. 3 (8 February 1968),
        39-40.
        New York, Greenwich Mews Theatre.

Soyinka, Wole

The Swamp Dwellers--Review of Production

1336   AKANJI, SANGODARE. Black Orpheus, No. 6 (November 1959),
       pp. 50-51.
           Produced at University College Ibadan by the Students
       Dramatic Society.

The Swamp Dwellers-Criticism

1337   MACLEAN, UNA, M. M. MAHOOD, and PHEBEAN OGUNDIPE. "Three
       Views of 'The Swamp Dwellers.'" Ibadan, No. 6 (June 1959),
       pp. 27-30.
           Includes discussion of theme and intended audience.

THREE PLAYS--Reviews

1338   AKANJI. Black Orpheus, No. 13 (November 1963), pp. 58-59.

1339   BANHAM, MARTIN. "Criticism of Soyinka's Three Plays." Books
       Abroad, 38, No. 1 (Winter 1964), 92.

1340   COOK, DAVID. "Of the Strong Breed." Transition, 3, No. 13
       (March-April 1964), 38-40.

1341   HOLMES, TIMOTHY. "Five Soyinka Plays." The New African, 2,
       No. 6 (13 July 1963), 112-13.

The Trials of Brother Jero--Reviews of Productions

1342   CLURMAN, HAROLD. Nation, 205, No. 19 (4 December 1967), 606.
           New York, Greenwich Mews Theatre.

1343   "Harsh Comedy on Lagos Beach." The Times (29 June 1966),
       p. 7.
           Hempstead Theatre Club.

1344   "Infectious Humanity." Time (17 November 1967), pp. 50, 52.
           New York, Greenwich Mews Theatre.

1345   JONES, D. A. N. New Statesman, 72, No. 1843 (8 July 1966),
       63-64.
           Hempstead Theatre Club.

1346   MACLEAN, UNA. "Three One-Act Plays." Ibadan, No. 9 (June
       1960), p. 21.
           University College Ibadan.

Soyinka, Wole

1347   NAGENDA, JOHN.   Cultural Events in Africa, No. 20 (July 1966),
       pp. III-IV.
       Hempstead Theatre Club.

1348   NWANKWO, NKEM.   Nigeria Magazine, No. 72 (March 1962), p. 80.
       Ibadan, Mbari Club.

1349   OLIVER, EDITH.   New Yorker, 43, No. 39 (18 November 1967),
       133-34.
       New York, Greenwich Mews Theatre.

1350   West Africa, No. 2916 (30 April 1973), pp. 563-64.
       Performed at British Council in Portland Place.

The Trials of Brother Jero--Criticism

1351   JABBI, BU-BUAKEI.   "The Form of Discovery in Brother Jero."
       Journal of the Nigeria English Studies Association, 7,
       Nos. 1-2 (December 1975), 43-50. Reprinted in Obsidian, 2,
       No. 3 (Winter 1976), 26-33.

1352   POVEY, JOHN F.   "Wole Soyinka: Two Nigerian Comedies." Com-
       parative Drama, 3, No. 2 (Summer 1969), 120-32.

1353   PRIEBE, RICHARD.   "Soyinka's Brother Jero: Prophet, Politi-
       cian, and Trickster." Pan African Journal, 4, No. 4
       (Fall 1971), 431-39. African Studies Association annual
       meeting paper, 1971.

1354   RICARD, ALAIN.   "Les Paradoxes de Wole Soyinka." Présence
       Africaine, No. 72 (1969), pp. 202-11.

AMOS TUTUOLA

1355   ACKERLY, NANCY.   "WLB Biography: Amos Tutuola." Wilson Li-
       brary Bulletin, 38, No. 1 (September 1963), 81.

1356   AFOLAYAN, A.   "Language and Sources of Amos Tutuola." In
       Perspectives on African Literature. Edited by Christopher
       Heywood. New York: Africana, 1971, pp. 49-63.

1357   "African Writers and Original Manuscripts." Afriscope, 4,
       No. 1 (January 1974), 55, 57.
       The loss of Tutuola's manuscripts.

1358   AGETUA, JOHN. "Interview with Amos Tutuola." In his <u>Inter-</u>
        <u>views with Six Nigerian Writers</u>. Benin City: Bendel
        Newspapers Corp., 1976?, pp. 4-8.

1359   AKINJOGBIN, I. ADEAGBO. "The Books of Amos Tutuola." <u>West</u>
        <u>Africa</u>, No. 1945 (5 June 1954), p. 513. Reprinted in
        <u>Critical Perspectives on Amos Tutuola</u>. Edited by Bernth
        Lindfors. Washington, D.C.: Three Continents Press, 1975,
        p. 41.
            Letter which asserts that Tutuola's works will be harm-
        ful to Europeans' view of Nigeria.

1360   ANOZIE, SUNDAY OGBONNA. "Amos Tutuola: littérature et folk-
        lore ou le problème de la synthèse." <u>Cahiers d'Etudes</u>
        <u>Africaines</u>, 10, No. 2 (1970), 335-51. Reprinted in his
        <u>Sociologie du roman africaine: Realisme, structure et dé-</u>
        <u>termination dans le roman moderne ouest-africain</u>. Paris:
        Aubier-Montaigne, 1970, pp. 65-88. Reprinted as "Amos
        Tutuola: Literature and Folklore, Or the Problem of Syn-
        thesis." In <u>Critical Perspectives on Amos Tutuola</u>. Edited
        by Bernth Lindfors. Washington, D.C.: Three Continents
        Press, 1975, pp. 237-53.

1361   AWOONOR, KOFI. "Amos Tutuola and Yoruba Folkore." In his
        <u>The Breast of the Earth</u>. Garden City, N.Y.: Anchor Press/
        Doubleday, 1975, pp. 226-50.

1362   BANJO, AYO. "Aspects of Tutuola's Use of English." In <u>Essays</u>
        <u>on African Literature</u>. Spectrum Monograph Series in the
        Arts and Sciences, 3. Edited by W. L. Ballard. Atlanta:
        School of Arts and Sciences, Georgia State University,
        1973, pp. 155-73.

1363   BOHANNAN, PAUL. "Translation: A Problem in Anthropology."
        <u>The Listener</u>, 60, No. 1315 (13 May 1954), 815-16.
            Tutuola's ability to translate Yoruba culture into the
        English language.

1364   CHAKAVA, HENRY M. "Amos Tutuola: The Unselfconscious Eccen-
        tric." <u>Busara</u>, 3, No. 3 (1971), 50-57.
            Tutuola's grammar, his unselfconsciousness, and his
        future as a writer.

1365   COLLINS, HAROLD R. <u>Amos Tutuola</u>. New York: Twayne, 1969.
        146 pp.

Tutuola, Amos

1366   COLLINS, HAROLD R.   "Founding a New National Literature: The
        Ghost Novels of Amos Tutuola."   Critique, 4, No. 1 (Fall-
        Winter 1960-1961), 17-28.   Reprinted in Critical Perspec-
        tives on Amos Tutuola.   Edited by Bernth Lindfors.
        Washington, D.C.:   Three Continents Press, 1975, pp. 59-70.
        Defends Tutuola's structure and characterization.

1367   COLLINS, HAROLD R.   "Nwoga's Magic Formula for the Criticism
        of Tutuola."   African Studies Association annual meeting
        paper, 1974.   [Not published, but available for purchase
        from African Studies Association.]

1368   COLLINS, HAROLD R.   "A Theory of Creative Mistakes and the
        Mistaking Style of Amos Tutuola."   World Literature Written
        in English, 13, No. 2 (November 1974), 155-71.
        On Tutuola's "incorrect" English usage.

1369   DATHORNE, O. R.   "Amos Tutuola: The Nightmare of the Tribe."
        In Introduction to Nigerian Literature.   Edited by Bruce
        King.   New York: Africana, 1972, pp. 64-76.

1370   DUSSUTOUR-HAMMER, MICHELE.   Amos Tutuola: Tradition orale et
        écriture du conte.   Paris: Présence Africaine, 1976.
        158 pp.

1371   EKO, EBELE OFOMA.   "The Critical Reception of Amos Tutuola,
        Chinua Achebe and Wole Soyinka in England and America
        1952-1974."   Dissertation, University of North Carolina at
        Greensboro, 1974.

1372   ENEKWE, OSSIE ONUORO.   "Amos Tutuola: An African Surrealist."
        Shantih, 3, No. 2 (1974-1975), 45.

1373   FERRIS, WILLIAM R.   "Folklore and the African Novelist:
        Achebe and Tutuola."   Journal of American Folklore, 86,
        No. 339 (January-March 1973), 25-36.

1374   IRELE, ABIOLA.   "Tradition and the Yoruba Writer: D. O.
        Fagunwa, Amos Tutuola and Wole Soyinka."   Odu, No. 11
        (January 1975), pp. 75-100.

1375   KING, BRUCE.   "Two Nigerian Writers: Tutuola and Soyinka."
        The Southern Review, 6, No. 3 (July 1970), 843-48.

1376   KLÍMA, VLADIMÍR.   "Tutuola's Inspiration."   Archiv Orientalni,
        35, No. 4 (1967), 556-62.   Reprinted in The East Under
        Western Impact.   Prague: Academia, 1969, pp. 121-28.
        Outside influences on Tutuola's works.

1377   LARRABEE, ERIC. "Amos Tutuola: A Problem in Translation."
        <u>Chicago Review</u>, 10, No. 1 (Spring 1956), 40-44.
        Aspects of Tutuola's culture which are reflected in his
        writing.

1378   LAURENCE, MARGARET. "A Twofold Forest." In her <u>Long Drums
        and Cannons: Nigerian Dramatists and Novelists</u>. New York:
        Praeger, 1969, pp. 126-47.
        Interpretative analysis of his works.

1379   LINDFORS, BERNTH. "Amos Tutuola and D. O. Fagunwa." <u>The
        Journal of Commonwealth Literature</u>, No. 9 (July 1970),
        pp. 57-65.
        Contrasts and compares Tutuola and Fagunwa.

1380   LINDFORS, BERNTH. "Amos Tutuola and His Critics." African
        Studies Association annual meeting paper, 1968. <u>Abbia</u>,
        No. 22 (May-August 1969), pp. 109-18.
        Tutuola has not received the scholarly research, by
        critics, that he deserves. Various critics' opinions are
        examined.

1381   LINDFORS, BERNTH. "Amos Tutuola: Debts and Assets." <u>Cahiers
        d'Etudes Africaines</u>, 10, No. 2 (1970), 306-34. Reprinted
        in his <u>Critical Perspectives on Amos Tutuola</u>. Washington,
        D.C.: Three Continents Press, 1975, pp. 275-306.
        Yoruba oral tradition and literary sources which in-
        fluenced Tutuola.

1382   LINDFORS, BERNTH. "Oral Tradition and the Individual Literary
        Talent." <u>Studies in the Novel</u>, 4, No. 2 (1972), 200-17.
        Reprinted in his <u>Folklore in Nigerian Literature</u>. New
        York: Africana, 1973, pp. 23-50.
        Combining of traditional and modern elements in the
        works of Tutuola, Nzekwu, and Achebe.

1383   LIYONG, TABAN LO. "Tutuola, Son of Zinjanthropus." <u>Busara</u>,
        1, No. 1 (1968), 3-8. Reprinted in his <u>The Last Word:
        Cultural Synthesis</u>. Nairobi: East African Publishing
        House, 1969, pp. 157-70. Reprinted in <u>Critical Perspec-
        tives on Amos Tutuola</u>. Edited by Bernth Lindfors.
        Washington, D.C.: Three Continents Press, 1975,
        pp. 115-22.

1384   MACKAY, MERCEDES. "The Books of Amos Tutuola." <u>West Africa</u>,
        No. 1941 (8 May 1954), p. 414. Reprinted in <u>Critical Per-
        spectives on Amos Tutuola</u>. Edited by Bernth Lindfors.
        Washington, D.C.: Three Continents Press, 1975, pp. 43-44.
        Letter which defends Tutuola from critics.

Tutuola, Amos

1385   McDOWELL, ROBERT E.   "Three Nigerian Storytellers: Okara,
       Tutuola, and Ekwensi."   Ball State University Forum, 10,
       No. 3 (Summer 1969), 67–75.
          The three authors' works have in common the influence of
       oral tradition and African characters without European
       contact.

1386   MEZU, S. OKECHUKWU.   "The Tropical Dawn (II):   Amos Tutuola."
       Nigerian Students Voice, 3, No. 1 (October 1965), 6–11.

1387   MOORE, GERALD.   "Amos Tutuola: A Modern Visionary."   In his
       Seven African Writers.   London: Oxford University Press,
       1962, pp. 39–57.

1388   MOORE, GERALD.   "Amos Tutuola."   Black Orpheus, No. 1
       (September 1957), 27–35.   Reprinted in Introduction to
       African Literature.   Edited by Ulli Beier.   Evanston, Ill.:
       Northwestern University Press, 1967, pp. 179–87.   Reprinted
       in Critical Perspectives on Amos Tutuola.   Edited by Bernth
       Lindfors.   Washington, D.C.:   Three Continents Press, 1975,
       pp. 49–57.
          The formal structure of Tutuola's novels is examined.

1389   NEUMARKT, PAUL.   "Amos Tutuola: Emerging African Literature."
       American Imago, 28, No. 2 (Summer 1971), 129–45.   Reprinted
       in Critical Perspectives on Amos Tutuola.   Edited by Bernth
       Lindfors.   Washington, D.C.:   Three Continents Press, 1975,
       pp. 183–92.

1390   NKOSI, LEWIS.   "Conversation with Amos Tutuola."   Africa
       Report, 9, No. 7 (July 1964), 11.   Reprinted as "African
       Writers of Today."   The Classic, 1, No. 4 (1965), 57–60.
          Interview.

1391   NYANG'AYA, ELIJAH.   "The Freakish Tutuola."   In Standpoints on
       African Literature.   Edited by Chris L. Wanjala.   Nairobi:
       East African Literature Bureau, 1973, pp. 188–96.

1392   OBIECHINA, E. N.   "Amos Tutuola and the Oral Tradition."
       Présence Africaine, No. 65 (1968), pp. 85–106.   Reprinted
       in Critical Perspectives on Amos Tutuola.   Edited by Bernth
       Lindfors.   Washington, D.C.:   Three Continents Press, 1975,
       pp. 123–44.

1393   OMOTOSO, KOLE.   "Interview with Amos Tutuola."   Afriscope, 4,
       No. 1 (January 1974), 62, 64.

1394   OWOMOYELA, OYEKAN. "Tutuola and His Critics: Thoughts on the
       Question of Language." African Studies Association annual
       meeting paper, 1974. [Not published, but available for
       purchase from African Studies Association.]

1395   "Portrait: A Life in the Bush of Ghosts." West Africa
       No. 1940 (1 May 1954), pp. 389-90. Reprinted in Critical
       Perspectives on Amos Tutuola. Edited by Bernth Lindfors.
       Washington, D.C.: Three Continents Press, 1975, pp. 35-38.
       Biographical.

1396   PRIEBE, RICHARD. "Tutuola, Fagunwa and Shakespeare." Journal
       of Commonwealth Literature, 8, No. 1 (June 1973), 110-11.
            A letter concerning Lindfors' comparisons of Tutuola and
       Fagunwa.

1397   PRIEBE, RICHARD. "Tutuola, the Riddler." African Studies
       Association annual meeting paper, 1974. In Critical Per-
       spectives on Amos Tutuola. Edited by Bernth Lindfors.
       Washington, D.C.: Three Continents Press, 1975,
       pp. 265-73.
            Tutuola's novels as riddles.

1398   REED, JOHN. "Folklore into Novel." Central African Examiner,
       6, No. 4 (September 1962), 27-28.
            Tutuola is praised for having put folk material into a
       modern form.

1399   ROBINSON, ERIC. "The Books of Amos Tutuola." West Africa,
       No. 1938 (17 April 1954), p. 344. Reprinted in Critical
       Perspectives on Amos Tutuola. Edited by Bernth Lindfors.
       Washington, D.C.: Three Continents Press, 1975, pp. 33-34.
            Letter which defends Tutuola's borrowing from folklore
       and his language.

1400   SODIPO, ADE. "The Books of Amos Tutuola." West Africa,
       No. 1945 (5 June 1954), p. 513. Reprinted in Critical
       Perspectives on Amos Tutuola. Edited by Bernth Lindfors.
       Washington, D.C.: Three Continents Press, 1975, p. 39.
            Letter which addresses controversy on merits of Tutuola.

1401   TAIWO, OLADELE. "Amos Tutuola." In his Culture and the
       Nigerian Novel. New York: St. Martin's Press, 1976,
       pp. 74-110.

1402   TAIWO, OLADELE. "The Essentials of Amos Tutuola's Narrative
       Art." Literary Half-Yearly, 17, No. 1 (January 1976),
       57-75.

Tutuola, Amos

1403 TAKACS, SHERRYL. "Oral Tradition in the Works of Amos
Tutuola." Books Abroad, 44, No. 3 (Summer 1970), 392-98.

1404 TUCKER, MARTIN. "Three West African Novelists." Africa
Today, 12, No. 9 (November 1965), 10-14.

AJAIYI AND HIS INHERITED POVERTY--Reviews

1405 AGBEBIYI, GLADYS. Nigeria Magazine, No. 96 (March 1968),
p. 53. Reprinted in Critical Perspectives on Amos Tutuola.
Edited by Bernth Lindfors. Washington, D.C.: Three Continents Press, 1975, p. 103.

1406 AWOONOR-WILLIAMS, GEORGE. West Africa, No. 2656 (27 April
1968), pp. 490-91.

1407 BALOGUN, OLA. Présence Africaine, No. 65 (1968), pp. 180-81.
Reprinted in Critical Perspectives on Amos Tutuola. Edited
by Bernth Lindfors. Washington, D.C.: Three Continents
Press, 1975, pp. 101-02.

1408 GOLDMAN, ARNOLD. The Listener, 78, No. 2020 (14 December
1967), 792. Reprinted in Critical Perspectives on Amos
Tutuola. Edited by Bernth Lindfors. Washington, D.C.:
Three Continents Press, 1975, p. 99.

1409 LINDFORS, BERNTH. "Nigerian Fiction of 1967." Journal of the
New African Literature and the Arts, Nos. 13-14 (1972),
pp. 71-72.

1410 MacNAMARA, DESMOND. New Statesman, 74, No. 1917 (8 December
1967), 819. Reprinted in Critical Perspectives on Amos
Tutuola. Edited by Bernth Lindfors. Washington, D.C.:
Three Continents Press, 1975, pp. 97-98.

1411 MORSBERGER, ROBERT E. Books Abroad, 42, No. 3 (Summer 1968),
492.

1412 Observer (31 December 1967), p. 20.

1413 THORPE, MICHAEL. English Studies, 49, No. 3 (June 1968), 273.

1414 Times Literary Supplement (18 January 1968), p. 53.

1415 WORDSWORTH, CHRISTOPHER. Manchester Guardian Weekly, 97,
No. 24 (14 December 1967), 11.

AJAIYI AND HIS INHERITED POVERTY--Criticism

1416   SCHMIDT, NANCY J.   "Tutuola Joins the Mainstream of Nigerian
       Novelists." Africa Today, 15, No. 3 (June-July 1968),
       22-24.
           Differences between Ajaiyi and Tutuola's other novels.

THE BRAVE AFRICAN HUNTRESS--Reviews

1417   AKANJI. Black Orpheus, No. 4 (October 1958), pp. 51-53.
       Reprinted in Critical Perspectives on Amos Tutuola. Edited
       by Bernth Lindfors. Washington, D.C.: Three Continents
       Press, 1975, pp. 83-85.

1418   BARO, GENE. "Nigerian Storyteller's Strange World." New York
       Herald Tribune Book Review (25 January 1959), p. 6.

1419   CLARKE, JOHN HENRIK. Présence Africaine, No. 26 (June-July
       1959), pp. 126-27.

1420   CROWDER, MICHAEL. West African Review, 29, No. 369 (June
       1958), 509.

1421   Manchester Guardian (1 April 1958), p. 4.

1422   NAIPAUL, V. S. New Statesman, 55, No. 1412 (5 April 1958),
       444. Reprinted in Critical Perspectives on Amos Tutuola.
       Edited by Bernth Lindfors. Washington, D.C.: Three Con-
       tinents Press, 1975, p. 87.

1423   SMITH, STEVIE. Spectator, 200, No. 6770 (28 March 1958),
       405.

1424   V., R. New York Times Book Review (2 November 1958), p. 41.

FEATHER WOMAN OF THE JUNGLE--Reviews

1425   ASCHERSON, NEAL. New Statesman, 63, No. 1626 (11 May 1962),
       683.

1426   D., S. D. "Two Views of Africa." West African Review, 33,
       No. 416 (August 1962), 57. Reprinted in Critical Perspec-
       tives on Amos Tutuola. Edited by Bernth Lindfors.
       Washington, D.C.: Three Continents Press, 1975, p. 93.

1427   DIPOKO, MBELLA SONNE. Présence Africaine, No. 44 (1962),
       p. 239. Présence Africaine, English ed., 16 (1962), 230.

Tutuola, Amos

1428   "The Mixture as Before." Times Literary Supplement (25 May
        1962), p. 369. Reprinted in Critical Perspectives on Amos
        Tutuola. Edited by Bernth Lindfors. Washington, D.C.:
        Three Continents Press, 1975, pp. 91-92.

1429   PRICE, R. G. G. Punch, 242, No. 6350 (23 May 1962), 805.

1430   RAVEN, SIMON. Spectator, 208, No. 6984 (4 May 1962), 597.

1431   Times Weekly Review (17 May 1962), p. 9.

MY LIFE IN THE BUSH OF GHOSTS--Reviews

1432   AMIS, KINGSLEY. Spectator, No. 6557 (26 February 1954),
        p. 244. Reprinted in Critical Perspectives on Amos Tutuola.
        Edited by Bernth Lindfors. Washington, D.C.: Three Con-
        tinents Press, 1975, pp. 25-26.

1433   BARO, GENE. "Adventures in Ghost Lands." New York Herald
        Tribune Book Review (28 November 1954), p. 2.

1434   DATHORNE, O. R. West African Journal of Education, 9, No. 1
        (February 1965), 55.

1435   HOLZHAUER, JEAN. "Primitive Dreams." Commonweal, 61, No. 1
        (8 October 1954), 23.

1436   JAMESON, R. D. Western Folklore, 14, No. 5 (October 1955),
        301-02.

1437   JOLAOSO, MABEL. Odu, No. 1 (January 1955), pp. 42-43.

1438   LEWIS, CECIL T. "Primitive Verbal Fantasy." Phylon, 16,
        No. 1 (1955), 117-18.

1439   MORGAN, WILLIAM. West African Review, 25, No. 327 (December
        1954), 1217.

1440   MURRA, JOHN V. "The Unconscious of a Race." Nation, 179
        (25 September 1954), 261-62.

1441   PRITCHETT, V. S. The New Statesman & Nation, 47, No. 1200
        (6 March 1954), 291. Reprinted in Critical Perspectives on
        Amos Tutuola. Edited by Bernth Lindfors. Washington, D.C.:
        Three Continents Press, 1975, pp. 21-23.

1442   QUIGLEY, ISABEL. Manchester Guardian (9 February 1954), p. 4.

1443   ROBINSON, ERIC. "Native Reserved Bush." West Africa,
       No. 1931 (27 February 1954), p. 179. Reprinted in Critical
       Perspectives on Amos Tutuola. Edited by Bernth Lindfors.
       Washington, D.C.: Three Continents Press, 1975, pp. 29-30.

1444   ROGOW, LEE. Saturday Review, 37, No. 46 (13 November 1954),
       57.

1445   S., H. V. L. African Affairs, 53, No. 213 (October 1954),
       348-49.

1446   THIAM, OUMAR DOUDOU. Présence Africaine, No. 51 (1964),
       pp. 178-79. Présence Africaine, English ed., 23 (1964),
       174-75.

1447   Times Literary Supplement (19 February 1954), p. 117.

MY LIFE IN THE BUSH OF GHOSTS--Criticism

1448   LINDFORS, BERNTH. "Amos Tutuola's Television-Handed Ghost-
       ess." Ariel, 2, No. 1 (January 1971), 68-77. Reprinted
       in his Folklore in Nigerian Literature. New York:
       Africana, 1973, pp. 61-72. Reprinted in Readings in Com-
       monwealth Literature. Edited by William Walsh. Oxford:
       Clarendon, 1973, pp. 142-51.
       Tutuola's Yoruba literary sources.

THE PALM-WINE DRINKARD--Reviews

1449   ASCHERSON, NEAL. New Statesman, 63, No. 1626 (11 May 1962),
       683.

1450   BARO, GENE. "Fantastic, Whimsical, Charming, Witty." New
       York Herald Tribune Book Review (20 December 1953), p. 6.

1451   CALDER-MARSHALL, ARTHUR. The Listener, 48, No. 1237
       (13 November 1952), 819. Reprinted in Critical Perspec-
       tives on Amos Tutuola. Edited by Bernth Lindfors.
       Washington, D.C.: Three Continents Press, 1975, pp. 9-10.

1452   EKWENSI, C. O. D. African Affairs, 51, No. 204 (July 1952),
       257-58. Reprinted in West African Review, 23, No. 298
       (July 1952), 713, 715.

1453   FREMANTLE, ANNE. "Magic." Commonweal, 58, No. 25
       (25 September 1953), 616.

Tutuola, Amos

1454 JACKSON, JOSEPH HENRY. "An African Gargantua." San Francisco
Chronicle (28 September 1953), p. 17.

1455 MORGAN, WILLIAM. West African Review, 23, No. 303 (December
1952), 1387.

1456 PRICE, R. G. G. Punch, 242, No. 6350 (23 May 1962), 805.

1457 RALEIGH, JOHN H. New Republic, 129, No. 20 (14 December
1953), 21.

1458 RODMAN, SELDEN. "Tutuola's World." New York Times Book Re-
view (20 September 1953), pp. 5, 29. Reprinted in Critical
Perspectives on Amos Tutuola. Edited by Bernth Lindfors.
Washington, D.C.: Three Continents Press, 1975, pp. 15-16.

1459 ROGOW, LEE. Saturday Review, 36, No. 42 (17 October 1953),
30, 44.

1460 "Search in Limbo." Times Literary Supplement (9 May 1952),
p. 309.

1461 TAYLOR, R. S. Library Journal, 78, No. 15 (1 September 1953),
1426.

1462 THOMAS, DYLAN. "Blithe Spirits." Observer (6 July 1952),
p. 7. Reprinted in Critical Perspectives on Amos Tutuola.
Edited by Bernth Lindfors. Washington, D.C.: Three Continents Press, 1975, pp. 7-8.

1463 WEST, ANTHONY. New Yorker, 29 (5 December 1953), 222-23.
Reprinted in Critical Perspectives on Amos Tutuola. Edited
by Bernth Lindfors. Washington, D.C.: Three Continents
Press, 1975, pp. 17-18.

THE PALM-WINE DRINKARD--Criticism

1464 AFOLAYAN, A. "Language and Sources of Amos Tutuola." In
Critical Perspectives on Amos Tutuola. Edited by Bernth
Lindfors. Washington, D.C.: Three Continents Press, 1975,
pp. 193-208.
A linguistic study.

1465 ANOZIE, SUNDAY OGBONNA. "Structure and Utopia in Tutuola's
The Palm-Wine Drinkard." The Conch, 2, No. 2 (September
1970), 80-88.
Analyzes the structure of the hero's conflict.

1466   ARMSTRONG, ROBERT P. "The Narrative and Intensive Continuity:
       The Palm-Wine Drinkard." Research in African Literatures,
       1, No. 1 (Spring 1970), 9-34. Reprinted in his The Affect-
       ing Presence: An Essay in Humanistic Anthropology.
       Urbana: University of Illinois Press, 1971, pp. 137-73.
       Reprinted in Critical Perspectives on Amos Tutuola. Ed-
       ited by Bernth Lindfors. Washington, D.C.: Three Con-
       tinents Press, 1975, pp. 209-35. Reprinted in Critical
       Perspectives on Nigerian Literatures. Edited by Bernth
       Lindfors. Washington, D.C.: Three Continents Press, 1976,
       pp. 101-29.

1467   ARNASON, D. "Amos Tutuola's The Palm-Wine Drinkard: The Na-
       ture of Tutuola's Achievement." Journal of Canadian Fic-
       tion, 3, No. 4 (1975), 56-59.

1468   EDWARDS, PAUL. "The Farm and the Wilderness in Tutuola's The
       Palm-Wine Drinkard." Journal of Commonwealth Literature,
       9, No. 1 (August 1974), 57-65. Reprinted in Critical Per-
       spectives on Amos Tutuola. Edited by Bernth Lindfors.
       Washington, D.C.: Three Continents Press, 1975, pp. 255-63.

1469   ENOBO KOSSO, MARTIN. "La Rencontre." Abbia, No. 25 (1971),
       pp. 28-68.

1470   JOHNSON, BABASOLA. "The Books of Amos Tutuola." West Africa,
       No. 1937 (10 April 1954), p. 322. Reprinted in Critical
       Perspectives on Amos Tutuola. Edited by Bernth Lindfors.
       Washington, D.C.: Three Continents Press, 1975, pp. 31-32.
          Letter which gives reasons why The Palm-Wine Drinkard
       "should not have been published at all."

1471   JONES, ELDRED. "Turning Back the Pages III: Amos Tutuola--
       The Palm-Wine Drinkard: Fourteen Years On." Bulletin of
       the Association for African Literature in English, No. 4
       (March 1966), pp. 24-30. Reprinted in Critical Perspec-
       tives on Amos Tutuola. Edited by Bernth Lindfors.
       Washington, D.C.: Three Continents Press, 1975, pp. 109-13.

1472   LARRABEE, ERIC. "Palm-Wine Drinkard Searches for a Tapster."
       The Reporter, 8, No. 10 (12 May 1953), 37-39. Reprinted in
       Critical Perspectives on Amos Tutuola. Edited by Bernth
       Lindfors. Washington, D.C.: Three Continents Press, 1975,
       pp. 11-14.
          Introduction to Tutuola, the man and his book.

Tutuola, Amos

1473   LARSON, CHARLES R.   "Time, Space, and Description: The
       Tutuolan World."   In his The Emergence of African Fiction.
       Bloomington: Indiana University Press, 1971, pp. 93–112.
       Reprinted in Critical Perspectives on Amos Tutuola.   Edited
       by Bernth Lindfors.   Washington, D.C.:   Three Continents
       Press, 1975, pp. 171–81.

1474   LINDFORS, BERNTH.   "Amos Tutuola's The Palm-Wine Drinkard and
       Oral Tradition."   Critique, 11, No. 1 (1968), pp. 42–50.
       Reprinted in his Folklore in Nigerian Literature.   New
       York: Africana, 1973, pp. 51–60.

1475   LINN, MICHAEL D.   "Degrees of Grammaticalness in Amos
       Tutuola's The Palm-Wine Drinkard."   African Studies Asso-
       ciation annual meeting paper, 1974.   [Not published, but
       available for purchase from African Studies Association.]

1476   OGUNDIPE, OMOLARA (OMOLARA LESLIE).   "The Palm-Wine Drinkard:
       A Reassessment of Amos Tutuola."   Présence Africaine,
       No. 71 (1969), pp. 99–108.   Reprinted in Ibadan, No. 28
       (July 1970), pp. 22–26.   Reprinted in Journal of Common-
       wealth Literature, No. 9 (July 1970), pp. 48–56.   Reprinted
       in Critical Perspectives on Amos Tutuola.   Edited by Bernth
       Lindfors.   Washington, D.C.:   Three Continents Press, 1975,
       pp. 145–53.
            Concentrates on Tutuola's language usage.

SIMBI AND THE SATYR OF THE DARK JUNGLE--Reviews

1477   EKWENSI, C. O. D.   West African Review, 27, No. 340 (January
       1956), 45.   Reprinted in Perspectives on Amos Tutuola.
       Edited by Bernth Lindfors.   Washington, D.C.:   Three Con-
       tinents Press, 1975, p. 79.

1478   MOORE, G. H.   Odu, No. 4 (1957?), pp. 44–47.

1479   NICHOLSON, MARJORIE.   African Affairs, 55, No. 218 (January
       1956), 62–63.

1480   Times Literary Supplement (21 October 1955), p. 617.   Re-
       printed in Critical Perspectives on Amos Tutuola.   Edited
       by Bernth Lindfors.   Washington, D.C.:   Three Continents
       Press, 1975, p. 77.

OBIORA UDECHUKWU

1481   THOMAS, PETER. "Two Voices from the Biafran War." Concerning
         Poetry, 4, No. 2 (1971), 10-17.
               The effects of the war on two Ibo poets, along with sev-
         eral of their poems written during that period.

KALU UKA

1482   LINDFORS, BERNTH. "Interview with Kalu Uka." In his Dem-Say:
         Interviews with Eight Nigerian Writers. Austin: African
         and Afro-American Studies and Research Center, University
         of Texas, 1974, pp. 69-76.

SAM UKALA

Whiteness is Barrenness--Review of Production

1483   WILKINSON, NICK. Omabe, No. 18 (January-February 1976),
         pp. 19-21.
               Student production at University of Nigeria, Nsukka.

ADAORA LILY ULASI

MANY THING BEGIN FOR CHANGE--Review

1484   N., M. "Nuances of the Colonial Scene." West Africa,
         No. 2862 (21 April 1972), p. 483.

MANY THING YOU NO UNDERSTAND--Reviews

1485   COLE, BARRY. Spectator, 224, No. 7408 (20 June 1970), 822.

1486   "Passage to Nigeria." Times Literary Supplement (18 June
         1970), p. 653.

1487   T., S. "Triumph of Tradition." West Africa, No. 2782
         (3 October 1970), pp. 1155-56.

1488   TAIWO, OLADELE. "Social Criticism." In his Culture and the
         Nigerian Novel. New York: St. Martin's Press, 1976,
         pp. 34-73.

Uzodinma, Edmund Chukuemeka Chieke

EDMUND CHUKUEMEKA CHIEKE UZODINMA

OUR DEAD SPEAK--Reviews

1489   BIDWELL, JULIE. Nexus, 1, No. 3 (January 1968), 42-43.

1490   LINDFORS, BERNTH. "Nigerian Fiction of 1967." Journal of the
        New African Literature and the Arts, Nos. 13-14 (1972),
        pp. 71-72.

OKOGBULE WONODI

1491   THOMAS, PETER. "Two Voices from the Biafran War." Concerning
        Poetry, 4, No. 2 (1971), 10-17.
            The effects of the war on two Ibo poets, along with sev-
        eral of their poems written during that period.

ICHEKE AND OTHER POEMS--Reviews

1492   ONYEJELI, BONA. "Horns, Rituals, Death and Dance." Nigeria
        Magazine, No. 84 (March 1965), pp. 63-64.

1493   TOLSON, MELVIN B. "Three African Poets." African Forum, 1,
        No. 3 (Winter 1966), 121-23.

1494   VINCENT, THEO. Black Orpheus, No. 18 (October 1965),
        pp. 58-59.

ICHEKE AND OTHER POEMS--Criticism

1495   THEROUX, PAUL. "Voices out of the Skull: A Study of Six
        African Poets." Black Orpheus, No. 20 (August 1966),
        pp. 41-58. Reprinted in Introduction to African Litera-
        ture. Edited by Ulli Beier. Evanston, Ill.: Northwestern
        University Press, 1967, pp. 110-31.

Anthologies of Nigerian Literature

ACHEBE, CHINUA AND OTHERS
THE INSIDER--Reviews

1496   HALL, K. G. "Stories of the Nigerian Civil War in The
        Insider." Bulletin of the Association for Commonwealth
        Literature and Language Studies, No. 10 (June 1972),
        pp. 71-77.

1497   "The Literature of Civil War." Times Literary Supplement
        (3 March 1972), p. 247.

ADEMOLA, FRANCES, ed.
REFLECTIONS: NIGERIAN PROSE AND VERSE--Reviews

1498   BANHAM, MARTIN. Books Abroad, 38, No. 2 (Spring 1964),
        210-11.

1499   EZE, MARK N. Central African Examiner, 7, No. 8 (February
        1964), 14.

1500   IZEVBAYE, D. S. Black Orpheus, 2, No. 7 (1971-1972), 53.

1501   PARKES, FRANK. West Africa, No. 2405 (6 July 1963),
        pp. 755, 757.

1502   PETERSON, W. M. West African Journal of Education, 7, No. 3
        (October 1963), 175.

1503   Times Literary Supplement (20 September 1963), p. 709.

AZUONYE, CHUKWUMA, ed.
NSUKKA HARVEST: POETRY FROM NSUKKA 1966-1972--Review

1504   W., K. "Igbo Studies and Poems." West Africa, No. 2915
        (23 April 1973), pp. 531-32.

BANHAM, MARTIN, ed.
NIGERIAN STUDENT VERSE--Reviews

1505   AKANJI, SANGODARE. Odu, No. 8 (October 1960), pp. 71-72.

1506   Books for Africa, 30, No. 4 (October 1960), 119-20.

1507   KAYPER-MENSAH, A. W. "Ibadan's Poets." West Africa, No. 2263
         (15 October 1960), p. 1171.

BASSIR, OLUMBE, ed.
AN ANTHOLOGY OF WEST AFRICAN VERSE--Review

1508   AKANJI. Black Orpheus, No. 3 (May 1958), pp. 58-59.

BEIER, ULLI, ed.
THREE NIGERIAN PLAYS--Review

1509   GRAHAM-WHITE, ANTHONY. Journal of the New African Literature
         and the Arts, Nos. 5-6 (Spring-Fall 1968), pp. 82-85.

THOMAS, PETER, ed.
POEMS FROM NIGERIA--Review

1510   WORKMAN, JILL. Black Orpheus, 2, No. 3 (1968), 47-48.

Index of Critics

Numbers refer to entries.

Title Index

Numbers refer to entries.

145

Title Index